The Curious Boy's Book of Exploration

The Curious Boy's Book of Exploration

Sam Martin

razor
bill

The Curious Boy's Book of Exploration

RAZORBILL

This edition published by the Penguin Group in the U.S.A. and Canada.

Other Penguin offices worldwide
Penguin Young Readers Group
345 Hudson Street, New York, New York 10014, U.S.A.
Penguin Group (USA) Inc., 375 Hudson Street, New York, New York 10014, U.S.A.
Penguin Group (Canada), 90 Eglinton Avenue East, Suite 700, Toronto, Ontario, Canada M4P 2Y3
(a division of Pearson Penguin Canada Inc.)
Penguin Books Ltd, 80 Strand, London WC2R 0RL, England
Penguin Ireland, 25 St Stephen's Green, Dublin 2, Ireland (a division of Penguin Books Ltd)
Penguin Group (Australia), 250 Camberwell Road, Camberwell, Victoria 3124, Australia
(a division of Pearson Australia Group Pty Ltd)
Penguin Books India Pvt Ltd, 11 Community Centre, Panchsheel Park, New Delhi - 110 017, India
Penguin Group (NZ), 67 Apollo Drive, Mairangi Bay, Auckland 1311, New Zealand
(a division of Pearson New Zealand Ltd)
Penguin Books (South Africa) (Pty) Ltd, 24 Sturdee Avenue, Rosebank, Johannesburg 2196, South Africa

Penguin Books Ltd, Registered Offices: 80 Strand, London WC2R 0RL, England

Conceived and produced by
Elwin Street Limited
144 Liverpool Road
London N1 1LA
United Kingdom
www.elwinstreet.com

Cover design by Tony Palmer © Penguin Group (Australia)
Internal design: Thomas Keenes
Illustrations: David Eaton
Planet images pages 47 to 49 reprinted by kind permission of NASA.

10 9 8 7 6 5 4 3 2 1

ISBN: 978-1-59514-207-8

Library of Congress Cataloging-in-Publication Data is available

Printed in China

This book is dedicated to my two curious sons,
Ford and Wren, the best explorers I know.

The completion of this book would not have been possible without the support and guidance of a number of people. My loving and wise wife Denise deserves most of the thanks, both for her encouragement and tireless work pursuing her own career while keeping our family in shoes and sandwiches. I'd also like to thank my editor Dan Mills for his understanding and direction. Lastly, a hearty shout out to Jason Miller and especially Jerry Fugit, whose own powers of discovery kept the end in sight. I hope all those who are young and young at heart can find the inspiration in these pages to discover life to the fullest.

Contents

Introduction 8

Chapter 1 – Experimenting 10

Magnet power 12 ✦ Soap power 14 ✦ Chromatography 16
Static electricity 19 ✦ Cabbage acid indicator 21 ✦ Bubble bomb 23
Science or magic? 25 ✦ Soda geyser 27 ✦ Density 28
Test your sense of smell 31 ✦ Moving water uphill 32
Measuring wind speed 33 ✦ Measuring air pressure 35
Making smoke bomb 36 ✦ Making a lava lamp 38

Chapter 2 – Fact gathering 40

How a computer works 42 ✦ How a telephone works 44 ✦ Prisms 45
Why the sky is blue 46 ✦ The Solar System 47 ✦ Modeling the Solar System 50
How wings work 52 ✦ Metamorphosis 53 ✦ Why leaves change color 55
Measuring a tree's age 57 ✦ Fingerprints 58 ✦ Plaster casts 60
Archeology 62 ✦ Latitude and longitude 66 ✦ Roman numerals 67
How an engine works 69

Chapter 3 – Constructing 72

A hovercraft 74 ✦ A compass 76 ✦ A sundial 78 ✦ Bottle music 80
Panpipes 82 ✦ A kaleidoscope 83 ✦ Table football 85 ✦ A jigsaw puzzle 88
Paper hats 90 ✦ Papier mâché 93 ✦ A whirligig 96 ✦ Puppets 97

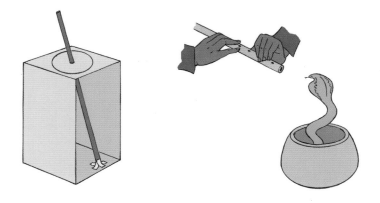

Chapter 4 – Tricking 100

Stink bombs 102 ✦ Balloon tricks 103 ✦ The jumping ping-pong ball 106
Putting your head through a postcard 107 ✦ The levitating teabag 109
The levitating olive 110 ✦ Pushing a glass through a table 111
Optical illusions 113 ✦ The classics 115 ✦ Mexican jumping beans 118
The ice hand 120 ✦ The pre-sliced banana 121 ✦ Cup and ball tricks 122
Number tricks 124 ✦ Card trick 127

Chapter 5 – Puzzling 128

Codes and ciphers 130 ✦ Crosswords 133 ✦ Finger cuffs 135 ✦ Riddles 136
Tangrams 138 ✦ Logic grids 140 ✦ Sudoku 142 ✦ More logic puzzles 144
Solitaire 146 ✦ Clock solitare 148 ✦ Rebuses 149 ✦ Paradoxes 151
Peg solitaire 153 ✦ Mazes 154 ✦ Word searches 155 ✦ Treasure hunts 156

Index 158

Introduction

❧❧❧

THERE WAS A TIME NOT TOO LONG AGO WHEN THE WORLD was a mystery. Sailors and explorers thought that if you traveled too far from shore you might fall off the end of the Earth into oblivion. Even after a few bold scientists proved that the world was round instead of flat, many thought that there was nothing but water between the shores of Western Europe and the Spice Islands of Southeast Asia. Boy, were they surprised to discover big hunks of land in between! The lands of the new world, Australia, New Zealand, and their surrounding islands were the cherries on the cake of this Age of Exploration.

These days, you would be hard pressed to find any area of land that hasn't already been mapped and measured, by satellite and on foot. But the Age of Exploration is far from over. Science is always pushing at the boundaries of human knowledge, the world of our curious minds. There's a whole universe of technology, science, and puzzles still waiting to be discovered. For the young and the young at heart, the Age of Exploration is alive and well.

Unfortunately, when most of us think of exploration, we think of TV shows. Or we might get excited about "discovering" the next level on the most recent video game. But do you ever wonder how that computer works? Why do you get an electric shock when you pick up the remote control? What if you could make your own games, or even your own movie with just a pad of paper and a pencil?

In this book, you will explore the reason why the sky is blue, how fingerprints are used to catch criminals, and how 300-ton passenger jets manage to fly instead of falling. Get crafty with papier mâché, learn how to play table football, and practice magic tricks. And for a dose of good old-fashioned mischief, cook up smoke bombs, or create a treasure hunt with cryptic clues and logic puzzles.

The continents of the world may all be mapped out and photographed, but exploring how the world works is the kind of fun any young adventurer can jump into any day of the week. And the good thing about this new Age of Exploration is that you don't need a sailboat or a crew of salty sailors to start. A curious mind will do just fine.

How to use this book

Some explorations are more difficult than others, and you might want a few extra hands to help out. Every activity is graded for difficulty by the number of scout badges underneath the title.

One-badge projects are for solo explorers. Two-badge projects might take a little more time and need someone else to help out. Three-badge projects are serious experiments.

⚠ Projects marked with this symbol involve elements that can be dangerous. If you don't know how to use these tools or elements, be sure to ask an adult before you start the project.

Chapter One

Experimenting

Sometimes the best way to explore is in the privacy of your own home laboratory, where you can put on some goggles and a pair of rubber gloves and mix up a potion.

✦

By playing chemist—or mad scientist—you get to collect all kinds of cool beakers and bottles. But more importantly, you get to find out how everything really works, from acids to electricity—and the truth is often pretty surprising! In fact, some of the experiments in this chapter are more like a magic show than science class. You can turn an egg into a mirror, create a bubble bomb, and make water flow uphill! Read on, and explore the hidden secrets of the lab.

Magnet power

❖

Playing with magnets is fun. At least it is for a while. But after the first few times, tricks like picking up a box-load of paper clips or sticking a picture to the refrigerator kind of lose their attraction. But what if you could use a magnet to power a boat?

It may sound silly, but magnet power will have your ship sailing in no time. Since the opposite poles of two magnets always pull toward each other, you can use the forces between them as a source of power for a small model craft. Follow these directions to weigh anchor like countless explorers before you. Remember, finding new uses for ordinary household items is what exploration is all about!

Like most of the activities in this book, the project is easy and can be done with regular household items (although one trip to the hardware store might help too). Give yourself about 30 minutes to complete it.

YOU WILL NEED

- A small wooden boat
- An eyelet screw
- A paper clip
- 2 small magnets
- Waterproof glue
- A rectangular glass baking dish
- Water

STEPS

1 SCREW THE EYELET SCREW into the middle of the bottom of the boat.

2 UNFOLD A PAPER CLIP and hook one end through the eyelet on the bottom of the boat.

3 THE REST OF THE PAPER CLIP SHOULD hang straight down from the boat—make sure it isn't too long or the boat won't fit in a shallow baking dish.

4 USE WATERPROOF GLUE to stick one magnet securely to the bottom of the paper clip.

5 ONCE THE GLUE IS DRY, fill a baking dish with water and float the boat in the dish. Make sure you use enough water so that the magnet stays just above the bottom of the dish.

> **WARNING**
>
> Don't leave your magnet in the water overnight, in case it starts to rust.

6 RUN A MAGNET SLOWLY ALONG THE OUTSIDE BOTTOM of the baking dish. It will attract the magnet suspended from the boat and pull the boat in any direction you want.

The top speed of your magnetic boat probably isn't that high. So you might be surprised to hear that scientists are working to develop a magnetic drive to power real ships through the water.

The drive works on a principle called "magnetohydrodynamics," and uses electricity running through saltwater in the presence of a magnetic field to create movement. Unfortunately, it's pretty slow at the moment—the only completed prototype was built in Japan in 1991 and could barely manage 9 miles per hour (15 kmph). In theory, however, a system like this could be used in the future to power ships reliably and efficiently. These engines would also be silent, which would make them ideal for powering submarines, which need to move very quietly so they don't give away their position.

DID YOU KNOW? The world's strongest permanent magnets (often called "supermagnets") are made from the alloy neodymium. A supermagnet the size of a quarter can be used to lift a weight of over 20 pounds (10 kg)!

Soap power

❖

Soap may be the most common thing in the house. Most of the time we use it to wash our hands or clean the dishes. But did you know it can power a paper boat too? That's because when soap is mixed with water it disrupts one of water's properties, known as surface tension.

Surface tension is what's responsible when you place a leaf or small piece of paper on top of water and it floats instead of sinking. That's because water is made up of hydrogen and oxygen atoms, which form molecules that stick very close together. The forces holding the molecules together essentially create a "skin" at the water's surface that prevents small objects from breaking through. That's surface tension. Some tiny bugs can float on water for the same reason (see next page).

The ingredients in soap can disrupt the forces that hold the water molecules together, and so dissolve the surface tension. This is how we can use soap to power a paper boat, by using soap to disrupt the surface tension on just one side of the model. All it takes is a little know-how.

YOU WILL NEED

- A sheet of card, stock paper, or an index card
- A pencil
- Scissors
- A rectangular glass baking dish
- Liquid soap

STEPS

1 ON THE CARD, DRAW OUT A FLAT BOAT with a pointed tip and round sides. It shouldn't be too large. Include a notch 1 inch (2.5 cm) across and ½ an inch (1.2 cm) deep in the back of the boat. Angle the sides of the notch outwards. This is where we're going to pour the liquid soap later.

2 CUT OUT THE BOAT along the lines you've drawn.

3 FILL A BAKING DISH with water.

4 PLACE THE FLAT BOAT ON TOP OF THE WATER at one end of the baking dish. The surface tension should hold it floating on top of the water.

5 PUT A FEW DROPS OF LIQUID SOAP in the notch at the back of the boat. The soap breaks down the surface tension of the water at the back of the boat, but not at the front or round the sides. Because there is an imbalance in the forces acting on the boat, it should be pushed gently forward.

6 YOU MUST CLEAN OUT THE BAKING DISH after each try or the boat won't move the next time.

Unlike magnetism, soap-power probably won't ever be used with life-sized ships. The forces produced by surface tension are too small and too easy to disrupt. But you can see surface tension in action in plenty of other places all around you. If you use an eye-dropper to gently place a drop of water on a smooth, flat surface like a glass table top, the drop will sit in the form of a round bead rather than spreading out thinly across the table. A drop of soapy water will spread out more than a drop of pure water, because the soap in the water disrupts the surface tension.

You can also use surface tension to make objects float that are denser than water, and should therefore sink (see page 28 for more on density). For example, a needle is made of metal, and metal sinks, right? But if you lay a needle gently on the surface of the water, surface tension will hold it up. Of course, if you add a little soap to the water . . . you can guess what happens.

DID YOU KNOW? Small bugs—often called water striders or pond skaters—can use surface tension to move across water without getting wet. Their only contact with the water is through their six legs, which are coated with wax, and covered in lots of tiny hairs that trap air and keep out moisture. Surface tension keeps these hairs from breaking through the water's surface, in spite of the weight of the bug, so that the insect can move around and prey on other, less agile creatures.

Chromatography

❖ ❖

Sometimes it seems as though scientific exploration is as much about learning big new words it is learning about the world. "Chromatography" is one of those words. It refers to the study of colored dyes.

You might wonder why scientists need to study color. After all, when something is green, it's green. Or is it? In fact, almost all colored dyes are made by mixing other colors together. Take a packet of sugar-coated candies, for example. Each color in that packet is a combination of dyes—all you have to do is look on the ingredients list to see how many. We can use chromatography to discover what dyes make up each color in a packet of candies, by dissolving the dyes and separating them out with a few simple household items. The experiment requires some patience and attention to detail, but can be done in about an hour.

YOU WILL NEED

- A packet of sugar-coated candies in different colors
- A paper coffee filter
- Scissors
- A sheet of tin foil
- Water
- An eye dropper
- 6 tall glasses
- Salt
- A ruler
- Tape
- 6 pencils
- 6 toothpicks
- A large empty soda bottle with a cap

STEPS

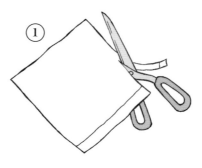

1 **CUT A RECTANGLE OUT OF YOUR PAPER COFFEE FILTER.** Using a ruler, measure a ¼ inch (6 mm) up from the bottom of the rectangle and draw a pencil line all the way across. Then cut the rectangle lengthways into 1-inch- (2.5-cm-) wide strips.

2 YOU SHOULD CUT AS MANY STRIPS as you have colors of candy, and each one should have a pencil line across the bottom.

3 JUST UNDER EACH LINE, USE YOUR PENCIL TO MAKE A DOT. Then label one dot for each different color of candy you have (for example, Y for yellow, G for green, BL for blue, BR for brown, R for red, and O for orange).

4 SET THE COFFEE FILTER STRIPS ASIDE and get out a sheet of tin foil. Using an eye dropper, put six drops of water on the foil. Space them far enough apart so that they don't run into each other.

5 NOW PUT A DIFFERENT COLORED CANDY ON EACH DROP OF WATER. After about a minute, the water will dissolve the colored dye off the candy. Once all the dye has come off the candies, carefully remove them so that you're left with colored drops of water.

6 NEXT, DIP THE TIP OF A TOOTHPICK INTO THE COLORED DROP and lightly touch it to the corresponding labeled dot on a coffee filter strip. You don't need much dye at all, so keep the dot of color small. Be sure to use a different toothpick for each color.

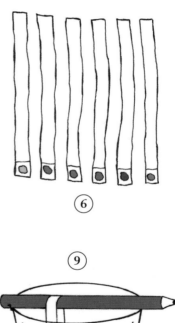

6

9

7 WAIT FOR THE SPOTS TO DRY and repeat step 6 two more times for each color, letting the spots dry each time before adding more dye.

8 WHEN THE SPOTS HAVE DRIED COMPLETELY, fold the top end of each strip over the middle of a pencil and tape it in place.

9 THEN BALANCE EACH PENCIL on top of a glass, so that the strip hangs down with the colored dots near the bottom of the glass.

10 CREATE A SALT "DEVELOPING" SOLUTION by mixing 3 cups (750 ml) water and 1 teaspoon salt in a large soda bottle. Shake the bottle until all the salt has dissolved.

11 POUR THE SALT SOLUTION INTO EACH GLASS until it just covers the bottom of each strip. Don't let the level of solution reach the colored dot, or it'll just wash off the dye.

12 HERE'S THE FUN PART: Watch as the filter absorbs the water, and the dots of dye begin to separate into the many colors used to make that dye up.

13 ONCE THE FILTERS HAVE ABSORBED ENOUGH WATER and the colors all seem to have separated, pull the strips out of the glasses and lay them on a table side by side to dry. Now you can see that the colors of each candy are actually made up of lots of different dyes.

Chromatography works because all the different colors in the dyes are made up of different-sized particles, some of which dissolve better than others in water. The water dissolves all the dyes together when it reaches the colored spot, but as the level of water creeps up, the water starts to evaporate off the paper. Because there is less water to carry them along, the dyes that are hardest to dissolve drop out of solution and stay on the paper, giving you a colored mark, while the rest of the colors move on. Each dye drops out at a different point, showing you clearly exactly what dyes have gone into the overall color.

If you are having trouble getting the colors to separate, you may need to give them more space. Try a longer piece of paper and a taller glass, and leave the process to work overnight. If you still can't see any colors separating out, then the dye probably only has one color in it.

DID YOU KNOW? The darker a dye is, the more different colors have probably gone into it. Dark blue and black dyes are usually made up of the most colors. This is because dyes work by absorbing wavelengths of light that our eyes see as color. Dark colors absorb more wavelengths than light colors, and mixing lots of different dyes together is an easy way to make sure more wavelengths are absorbed. (See pages 45 and 46 for more detail on how colors work.)

Static electricity

Shuffle your feet across a nylon-carpeted floor, and you get a shock when you touch a door knob. Rub a balloon on your head and your hair stands on end, while the balloon will stick to the wall. What's the connection? It's called static electricity. Static electricity is created when an object loses its electrical balance.

Everything in the universe is made up of tiny particles called atoms, which are themselves made up of even tinier particles called protons, electrons, and neutrons. Protons have a positive electrical charge, electrons a negative one, and neutrons have no charge at all. Even our own bodies are made up of these charged particles — the reason we don't go around sparking like frayed electrical wires is because the negative and positive charges in us offset each other, giving us (and most other objects) a neutral charge overall.

Static electricity is created when the balance gets out of whack. When two objects are rubbed together the electrons in one can sometimes jump to the other, causing the object that lost the electrons to become positively charged, and the object that gained the electrons to become negatively charged. This separation of charged particles is called static electricity.

So why do you get a shock if you touch a door knob after walking across the carpet? Because some of the electrons in the rug have jumped to you, giving you a small negative charge. When you touch the door knob, the shock you feel is the energy released by extra electrons in your body moving to the neutral door knob.

Your hair stands on end when you rub a balloon on it for a slightly different reason. Opposite electrical charges attract, and similar electrical charges push away from each other, just like the poles on a magnet. The friction of rubbing causes some of the electrons in your hair to jump to the balloon, giving each hair on your head a positive charge. That causes each hair to try and get away from the others, and the farthest away they can get is to stand up straight.

You can see the same process in other experiments. In this one, for example, you can use static electricity to bend a stream of water.

YOU WILL NEED:
- A plastic hair comb
- A water faucet

STEPS

1 TURN ON THE WATER FAUCET to get a small stream of water. The thinner the stream, the easier it'll be to make it bend.

2 RUN THE COMB THROUGH YOUR HAIR about five times. Some of the electrons from your hair will transfer to the comb, giving it a negative charge (your hair will likely stand up with repelling positive charges).

3 CAREFULLY BRING THE COMB CLOSE TO THE STREAM OF WATER, but don't let them touch. The negative charge of the comb will attract the positive charge of the water molecules, thereby bending the stream of water toward the comb.

4 IF THE WATER TOUCHES THE COMB, the static charge will dissipate and the effect will be lost.

If you can't get a charge off your hair, try stroking the comb with a fleece jacket to build up static.

Thunder and lightning are caused by static electricity. If you build up a big static charge, you can hear a crackling noise and see a small flash when it discharges. (Try taking off a woolen sweater or fleece in a dark room and you'll be able to see the flashes.) Thunder and lightning are exactly the same, only much, much bigger. The static charge is thought to be caused by water and ice particles in thunder clouds colliding and transferring electrons.

DID YOU KNOW? Photocopiers use static electricity to attach toner powder to the page in the form of the image that's being copied. They then fix the powder to the page by heating it.

Cabbage acid indicator

⚜ ⚜

Lots of everyday materials fall into one of two opposite categories: acids and bases. Knowing how acidic or basic a substance is can be important for a variety of reasons — for example, farmers have to know the acidity of their soil, because certain plants grow well in acidic soils while others prefer basic.

For these reasons, chemists have created a number of ways to test the acidity of materials. In 1909, a Danish chemist called Søren Sørensen came up with a numbered scale called "pH," which rates a substance from 1 (very acidic) through 7 (neutral) to 14 (very basic).

One neat way to test the acidity of substances around your house is to use chopped up cabbage. Chemists have discovered that cabbage juice contains a pigment which changes color at different pH levels. Something that's very acidic will turn red when mixed with cabbage juice, a neutral substance will be purple, and a basic substance will be greenish yellow.

DID YOU KNOW? Some of the earliest experiments on acids and bases came about because people noticed that cabbages grew red in some soils, but purple or blue in others.

Here's the color scale for the cabbage indicator:

pH	2	4	6	8	10	12
Color	Red	Purple	Violet	Blue	Blue-green	Green-yellow

To test things around your house for their level of acidity, all you need is half a head of red cabbage and an hour or so. Don't forget to grab a notebook so you can record what you discover.

YOU WILL NEED ⚠️

- Half a head of red cabbage
- A knife
- Boiling water
- A large glass bowl
- 5 to 10 small bowls

- A variety of household chemicals you want to test, like lemon juice, vinegar, baking soda, soap, and ammonia

STEPS

1 BOIL AT LEAST 2 CUPS (500 ml) of ordinary tap water.

2 CHOP UP ENOUGH CABBAGE to half fill the large glass bowl. Chop it as finely as you can.

3 POUR THE BOILING WATER OVER THE CHOPPED CABBAGE and let it sit for 10 minutes. The water should take on a purplish-blue color—it's kind of like making tea from cabbage.

4 AFTER 10 MINUTES, pour a small amount of liquid into each of the smaller bowls. Don't let any of the actual cabbage get in the bowls. This liquid is your indicator—the blue-purple color means it's neutral.

5 ADD A SMALL AMOUNT OF EACH HOUSEHOLD ITEM to the different bowls of indicator until the color of the water changes.

6 REFER TO THE ACID-COLOR SCALE on page 21 to determine the pH of each substance.

7 ACIDS AND BASES ALSO REACT TOGETHER and cancel each other out. Find an acidic solution and add a little of it to a basic solution with indicator in it. You should see the color of the solution change slowly back toward neutral.

DID YOU KNOW? Your stomach contains a powerful acid that helps you digest your food. It's mostly hydrochloric acid with a pH of about 2, which is enough to break down food for your body to absorb, and to kill some of the nasty bugs that might otherwise give you food poisoning.

Bubble bomb

❖

Experimenting with household materials and substances wouldn't be any fun if your mixtures didn't sometimes produce a reaction. Of course, some chemists have blown up their labs by combining the wrong things — we won't go that far. Here's a way we can cause some harmless commotion.

All you need for this experiment are a few basic items from the kitchen. The effect is almost instantaneous.

YOU WILL NEED

- Vinegar
- Baking soda
- Warm water
- A zip-lock bag
- Scissors
- Paper towel
- A measuring cup
- Measuring spoons

STEPS

1 PICK A GOOD OUTDOOR SPOT TO DO THE EXPERIMENT. Either that or make sure neither you nor anyone else minds that everything is going to get wet.

2 MAKE SURE YOUR BAG HAS NO HOLES IN IT. You can fill it up with water first as a test.

3 USING SCISSORS, CUT A PAPER TOWEL into four equal-sized squares.

4 PUT 1½ TABLESPOONS (20 ML) OF BAKING SODA in the middle of one square and fold all four sides of the paper towel over the baking soda. This is going to go into the vinegar — the paper stops the baking soda getting out right away, so you've got time to get clear. Pouring baking soda directly into the vinegar won't give you enough time to close the bag.

5 FILL THE BAG WITH ½ CUP (125 ML) VINEGAR and 1 cup (200 ml) warm water.

6 DROP YOUR BAKING SODA/PAPER TOWEL PACKET into the solution and quickly zip the bag closed.

7 PLACE THE BAG DOWN CAREFULLY and quickly stand back.

8 THE VINEGAR AND THE BAKING SODA PRODUCE A CHEMICAL REACTION that forms bubbles of carbon dioxide. As the gas in the bubbles expands, it creates pressure that will eventually pop the bag!

This is a classic example of a chemical reaction. Chemical reactions are when two chemicals combine to create new substances. Vinegar is a weak acid (known as "acetic acid"), and baking soda contains a chemical called sodium bicarbonate. Acids react with bicarbonates to create carbon dioxide gas, water, and a salt—in this case a chemical called sodium acetate. For chemists, a salt isn't just something to put on food—it's a substance that's made when an acid is neutralized in a chemical reaction.

The part we're interested in is the carbon dioxide gas: because we've sealed the bag shut, the gas creates pressure as it's given off. When the pressure is high enough, the bag can't contain it any longer and bursts.

DID YOU KNOW? Sodium acetate doesn't do much in our experiment, but it has its uses in industry—for making textiles and synthetic rubber, and preserving food. It's also used to make heating pads for hikers: a special solution of sodium acetate is kept in a plastic packet. When a metal tab inside the packet is flicked, it causes the solution to crystalize and give off heat, so cold trekkers and explorers can warm their hands and feet.

Science or magic?

One of the great things about discovering the secrets of science is that you can use what you know to impress and entertain your friends. In fact, some experiments would go down just as well on the magician's stage as in the lab. Two great examples are the egg mirror and the ice-cube-match pick-up. The results might seem mystical, but true explorers know that the secret is science.

Turning an egg into a mirror

Transform a regular hard-boiled egg into a shiny egg-shaped mirror with three simple steps. If you want a quick trick, do the first two steps ahead of time.

YOU WILL NEED

- A candle
- Tongs
- A hard-boiled egg, peeled
- Matches
- A glass of water

STEPS

1 LIGHT YOUR CANDLE and hold the peeled hard-boiled egg over the flame with some tongs until it begins to blacken with soot. Keep the egg over the flame until it's completely covered in soot. Don't let the egg burn — it'll smell bad and spoil the trick.

2 WHEN THE EGG IS COMPLETELY COVERED IN BLACK, set it aside to cool for a few minutes while you gather your audience.

3 IMMERSE THE EGG COMPLETELY in a glass of water, and watch as it turns silver and shiny like a mirror!

The secret? The soot (a thin layer of carbon particles) traps a film of air bubbles around the surface of the egg when you submerge it. The surface of the water around the film of air reflects light just like a mirror, making the egg appear shiny.

Picking up an ice cube with a match

When you announce to your friends that you plan to pick up an ice cube with a match, they'll probably think you've figured out a way to balance the cube on top of the match. Actually, it's much easier than that.

YOU WILL NEED
- A small bowl
- Water
- An ice cube
- Salt
- A match

STEPS

1 FILL THE BOWL WITH WATER and float an ice cube in it.

2 LAY THE MATCH ON TOP OF THE CUBE. Be sure to leave a small portion of the match hanging off the side so you'll be able to grab it later.

3 POUR SALT ON TOP of the ice cube around the match.

4 WAIT 3 MINUTES, then grab the match and pick it up, along with the ice cube stuck to it.

The secret? Water normally freezes at 32°F (0°C). But when you dissolve salt in water, it won't freeze until it reaches 20°F (-7°C). When you sprinkle salt onto the top of the ice cube, it dissolves a little and melts the top of the cube by lowering the temperature at which water turns to ice. However, once the ice on top of the cube has melted, the salt washes off into the bowl of water and the top of the ice cube quickly re-freezes, trapping the matchstick so it sticks to the ice.

One of the dangers of seas near the North and South Poles is that the salt in the water means they can stay liquid at very low temperatures. Anybody falling into the water loses their body heat very quickly, which can be fatal.

Soda geyser

✦

One of the great things about science is it's always advancing. Copernicus may never have done this soda experiment but it's still exciting. It's also pretty messy, so make sure you're wearing old clothes when you try it.

This experiment was first discovered by putting mint-flavored candies into soda, but table salt works just as well if not better. All you need is a wide open space, a few groceries, and a willingness to get wet.

YOU WILL NEED
- A bottle of diet soda
- Table salt
- A sheet of paper
- A big outdoor space

STEPS

1 TAKE ALL YOUR INGREDIENTS outside and away from anything that you don't want to cover in diet soda. This is a messy experiment.

2 ROLL THE PIECE OF PAPER loosely into a tube and pour a good handful of salt into it. Hold one end of the tube to keep the salt in.

3 TAKE THE CAP OFF the bottle. From arm's length, hold the tube over the bottle and funnel all the salt into the soda.

4 TRY AND RUN AWAY before the geyser covers you in soda!

Bubbles in soda are made by dissolving carbon dioxide gas in water used to make the drink. When salt or candies enter the soda, they cause all the carbon dioxide to come out of solution very quickly, shooting out of the bottle in a foamy jet.

WARNING

Never try this experiment with the cap on the bottle—apart from making a mess as you put the cap on, there's a danger that bits of the bottle or cap might burst and injure someone.

Density

Density is a scientific term that refers to the amount of mass an object contains relative to its size or volume. The more mass an object contains in a given space, the more dense it is. Something very heavy that occupies a small space, like an iron ball, is more dense than something very light that occupies a large space, like a pile of feathers.

You can calculate the density of an object by dividing its mass (weight) by its volume (the amount of space it occupies). Scientists have figured out various clever ways of working this out. One of these is to look at whether objects float or sink in different liquids. If an object is less dense than the liquid it's in, it will always float, and if it's more dense it will sink.

To discover how dense various substances are around your house, we can do a simple experiment involving water, syrup (which is denser than water), and cooking oil (which is less dense than water).

YOU WILL NEED

- A glass jar
- Water
- Syrup
- Cooking oil
- Small objects to test for density

STEPS

1 COLLECT SOME OBJECTS you want to test from around the house, such as plastic toys, coins, a grape, a cork, a piece of wood, etc.

2 FILL THE JAR UP ONE-THIRD FULL OF SYRUP. Then pour water on top to fill the jar up to two-thirds full. Then add oil so the jar is filled up all the way.

3 LET THE LIQUIDS SETTLE. The water should float on the syrup, and the oil should float on top of both. When they've formed three distinct layers, you're ready to begin.

4 GENTLY DROP VARIOUS HOUSEHOLD OBJECTS into the jar and record which layer they float in. A copper coin, for example, might be more dense than water and cooking oil but less dense than syrup. A grape will float on water, but probably sink in oil. Make a record of your findings.

The Cartesian Diver

Another density experiment is called the Cartesian Diver. This one uses water and air pressure to change the density of an object, and make it float or sink.

YOU WILL NEED
- A large empty soda bottle
- Modeling clay
- A pen cap
- Water
- A large bowl

STEPS

1 MAKE A MARBLE-SIZED BALL OF CLAY and stick it to the bottom of the pen cap. Block off any holes in the top of the cap with clay, so that water can't get in through the top. This will be your "diver."

2 TEST TO SEE IF THE DIVER FLOATS by putting him in a large bowl of water. If the diver sinks, remove some clay from the ball. If he lies flat on the surface, put a little more clay on the ball. The goal is to have just the tip of the pen cap sticking up out of the water.

3 ONCE YOU GET THE CLAY BALL JUST THE RIGHT SIZE, remove the labels from a large soda bottle, wash it out, and fill it all the way to the brim with water. Lower the diver in and screw on the cap. There should be no extra air inside the bottle, so your diver sits right under the cap.

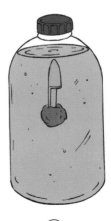

4 NOW GENTLY SQUEEZE THE SIDES OF THE BOTTLE. The diver in the bottle should begin to sink. Release the bottle and it will float back to the top.

(4)

5 WHEN YOU SQUEEZE THE BOTTLE, you are compressing the volume inside, including the volume of the air trapped in the pen cap. This compression pushes the air molecules in the pen cap together so the same weight occupies a smaller space, making the diver more dense than the water around and causing him to sink.

DID YOU KNOW? This experiment is named after René Descartes (think "Decartesian"). It is also sometimes called the Cartesian Devil, because it seems to have a mind of its own.

Density and ships

Density sometimes causes explorers to become confused. For example, metal is more dense than water, so it sinks. But a steel battleship can still float on the surface. How can that be possible?

The answer is that a ship is only a steel shell, and inside the shell are rooms full of air. Because air is much less dense than water (which is why air bubbles always quickly rise to the surface) it reduces the overall density of the ship and keeps it afloat.

When water gets into a ship, for example through a hole in the hull, it replaces the air, increasing the ship's overall density and causing it to begin to sink. If too much water gets in, the ship will become denser than the surrounding water and will sink to the bottom.

Submarines use this principle to alter their depth underwater. Submarines are equipped with huge air tanks that make them float on the surface like a normal ship. When the captain wants to submerge, the order is given for the air in the tanks to be pumped into another space (where it's usually kept compressed so it takes up less space, like the air in your Cartesian Diver) and the air tanks to be filled with water. By pumping different amounts of water into the tanks, submarines can be made more or less dense so they can float or sink as needed.

Test your sense of smell

❖

Ever wonder how many smells there are in the world? Scientists have, and they've found out that people can detect up to 10,000 different smells. Our noses contain about 40 million tiny hairs called "cilia" to detect the chemicals that make up odors.

The people that can sniff out 10,000 different smells are actually the lucky ones — or maybe the unlucky ones. Some people can only detect 3,000 smells, and some can't smell at all! To discover how good your or your friends' sense of smell is, try this test.

YOU WILL NEED
- A shoebox
- A screw driver
- A notebook and pen
- Various smelly things

STEPS

1 COLLECT A NUMBER OF DIFFERENT SMELLY THINGS from around the house, like lemon or orange peel, cedar wood, coffee grinds, cocoa, garlic, vanilla, etc.

2 MAKE A FEW HOLES IN THE LID OF A SHOEBOX with a screwdriver. To test your own sense of smell, have a friend secretly place one of the items you've collected from around the house in the box and close the lid.

3 TAKE A SNIFF, and in a notebook write down what you think it is. Rate the odor of each item on a scale of 1 to 10, for how strong it is and whether it's a good or bad smell. Write down any memories you associate with each smell as well.

4 HAVE YOUR FRIEND SHOW YOU THE OBJECT to see if you identified it correctly. Then switch places and make a note of his results.

DID YOU KNOW? Human's might have 40 million smell detectors in their noses but dogs have 2 billion!

Moving water uphill

❖

If you do enough experiments you'll start to wonder if anything is really as it seems. Luckily, there are a few natural rules that won't ever change. Take water. It will always flow downhill, right? Wrong. In certain situations water can actually flow upward!

How do you think trees get water from the ground all the way up to their leaves? They do it by a process called capillary action. A capillary is a tiny tube about the width of a piece of hair. When liquid enters into these tiny tubes, it is drawn along their length. You can see the effect for yourself in about 10 minutes by gathering a few ingredients together.

YOU WILL NEED

- A tall glass
- Water
- Food coloring
- Clear plastic tubing of various diameters, from pencil-thickness to the thinnest you can find

STEPS

1 FILL A GLASS HALF FULL WITH WATER, and add a few drops of food coloring so you can see the water level clearly.

2 PUT ONE END OF THE LARGEST CLEAR PLASTIC TUBE in the glass of water and watch as the level of water in the tube rises a little.

3 NOW TRY THE THINNER TUBES. The water should climb higher the thinner the tubes get. If you want to imagine how high the water could climb if the tubes were hair-thin, look at the height of a tree!

DID YOU KNOW? The world's tallest living tree is a redwood in California called Hyperion. It is 379 feet (156 m) tall.

Measuring wind speed

❧❧

Wind is always around us, whether it's a gentle breeze that just rustles the leaves or a hurricane that threatens to tear the roofs off our houses. Wind is always gusting around the globe. But where does it come from? What is wind?

Wind is the movement of air across the surface of the Earth. It happens because of shifts in air pressure (see page 35), which changes according to the temperature, and the movement of the Earth spinning on its axis. Wind is what we feel when air shifts from an area of high pressure to an area of low pressure.

Lots of people depend on wind for their work and their experiments. Weather scientists (or meteorologists) check the wind to give weather forecasts; pilots constantly check wind patterns when they're flying; and sailors, even on boats with engines, always have to know when the wind is coming and which way it's going to blow.

There are lots of different ways to check wind speed. Scientists use instruments called "anemometers," which come in a variety of different designs. Simple ones have a propellor blade or a series of cups mounted on a wheel, which spin in the wind. The instrument measures how fast they're spinning and uses that data to calculate the wind speed.

One easy experiment for measuring wind speed without an anemometer is to use a ping-pong ball suspended on the end of a string. Setting this one up shouldn't take more than 10 minutes. Then you have to wait for the leaves to start rustling.

YOU WILL NEED

- A ping-pong ball
- 10 inches (25 cm) of string
- A protractor
- Sticky tape
- A notebook and pen

STEPS

1 TAPE ONE END OF THE STRING to the ping-pong ball, and tape the other end to the center point of the protractor's straight edge.

2 FIND A SPOT OUT IN THE OPEN where the wind won't be blocked by trees or buildings.

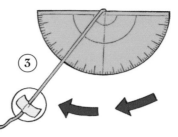

3 HOLD THE PROTRACTOR UPSIDE-DOWN, so the string hangs down across the face. Stand with your back to the wind and let the string and the ping-pong ball hang in the wind. The wind will blow the ping-pong ball out sideways so that the string will be pulled at an angle across the protractor.

4 USE THE WIND-SPEED SCALE BELOW to determine how fast the wind is moving. The stronger the wind, the sharper (or smaller) the angle will be. If there's no wind at all the ball will hang straight down, so the protractor will read a 90-degree angle.

5 RECORD WIND SPEEDS OVER THE COURSE OF A DAY, making sure to also record the time each measurement was taken. You may want to take note of the weather and temperature at the time of your measurements, and see if any patterns or relationships can be found.

6 IF YOU RECORD THE DIRECTION the wind was blowing from along with the wind speed, by taking a compass with you (see page 76), you can add that to your list of data. Bad weather often blows in from the same direction — use your data to work out which direction that is around your home.

Wind Speed Scale
90° = 0 mph (0 kmph)
83° = 6 mph (10 kmph)
75° = 10 mph (16 kmph)
61° = 15 mph (24 kmph)
50° = 18 mph (29 kmph)
45° = 19.5 mph (31 kmph)
35° = 23.5 mph (38 kmph)
20° = 32.5 mph (52 kmph)

Measuring air pressure

✦ ✦

Along with wind speed, explorers need to know about air pressure. Low pressure means wind and rain, and high pressure means warm days in summer, and cold days in winter.

Meteorologists use an instrument called a "barometer" to measure air pressure. You can construct a simple one by yourself very easily.

YOU WILL NEED

- A glass jar
- A balloon
- A drinking straw
- Glue
- A piece of card
- A fine-tipped pen or sharp pencil

STEPS

1 CUT A CIRCLE OUT OF THE BALLOON and stretch it over the top of the jar to create a tight seal, like a drum. Carefully stick one end of the straw to the middle of the balloon, so the rest of the straw pokes out over the side of the jar.

2 GLUE ONE EDGE of the cardboard to the side of the jar so that the straw sticks out across it. Mark the exact position of the straw on the card. Check the straw every day and mark its new position on the card.

When you stretch the balloon over the jar, you seal air inside at whatever the air pressure is at that moment. If the air pressure outside the jar drops, the membrane will swell, because the pressure inside will be higher by comparison. This will push the tip of the straw down. If the air pressure rises, the pressure inside the jar will be relatively low, and the membrane will sag inward, pushing the tip of the straw up.

WARNING

The straw will probably only move a very small amount. Make sure your marks are very accurate so you can spot the differences.

Making smoke bombs

✦✦

A more messy (and fun!) way to test which direction the wind is blowing is to fill the air with smoke from a smoke bomb. And it's all in the name of chemistry. This isn't a difficult experiment. Most of the ingredients can be found around the house, although one of the most important ones—potassium nitrate, also known as saltpeter—needs to come from a garden supply store. You can get fuses from a hobby store—they're usually referred to as "safety" or "hobby" fuses.

Give yourself about an hour to mix, mold, and cool the smoke bombs.

YOU WILL NEED
- 1 cup (200 g) sugar
- 1 ½ cups (300 g) potassium nitrate
- A skillet
- A stove
- Tin foil
- Fuses
- Matches

⚠

STEPS

1 MIX THE SUGAR AND POTASSIUM NITRATE together in a bowl. You'll need about three parts potassium nitrate to two parts sugar.

2 PUT YOUR SKILLET ON THE STOVE over a low heat, and pour in the sugar-potassium nitrate mixture.

3 STIR THE MIXTURE AND HEAT IT VERY GENTLY until the sugar begins to caramelize and turn a brown color. If it starts turning black, immediately remove the skillet from the heat.

4 ONCE THE INGREDIENTS HAVE TURNED GOOEY and brown, spoon out small globs onto a sheet of tin foil, spacing each one about 2 inches (5 cm) apart.

5 PUSH FUSES INTO THE MIDDLE of each glob and leave them to dry.

6 WHEN ALL THE MIXTURE HAS BEEN SPOONED OUT, put the skillet in the sink and fill it with hot water, otherwise the sugar and potassium nitrate will stick to the pan like concrete and be very difficult to clean. Be sure to wipe up any spills too before they harden.

WARNING

Always be careful when heating chemicals and using matches. Always place smoke bombs in clear, open places away from dry grass and leaves — sparks from the fuse can ignite dry underbrush.

7 LET THE SMOKE BOMBS COOL and harden for at least three hours. Then you can take them outside and light them!

8 PUT A MATCH TO THE FUSE and stand back. When the heat reaches your mixture, it should start to give off clouds of white smoke.

9 TAKE NOTE OF HOW FAST OR SLOW your smoke bombs are burning. If the sugar-potassium nitrate mix is too sugary, they will be hard to light and will burn slowly. Too much potassium nitrate will make them burn too quickly and too hot, which means less smoke.

Burning is another chemical reaction, this time between a fuel and oxygen in the atmosphere. Smoke is simply clouds of tiny particles, caused by the reaction, which the hot air rising from the fire carries upward. In this case, most of the smoke is actually steam caused by a chemical reaction between oxygen and sugar.

DID YOU KNOW? Smoke bombs are used in the military. Devices that emit large clouds of colored smoke are used to mark out areas for helicopters to land, or supplies or troops to be parachuted in. And devices that emit clouds of white smoke are used to confuse enemy soldiers by blocking their vision. Smoke canisters are also used by formation-flying display aircraft to draw patterns in the sky and entertain people on the ground.

Making a lava lamp

❖

With this project you not only get to explore the different properties of oil and water but you get to create a cool new decoration for your room. Real lava lamps were invented in 1963 in England by a man named Craven Walker. They were popular in the 1960s and 70s, but by the 80s they lost their appeal—at least for some. Others have always enjoyed watching globs of goo float up and down under a red or purple light.

To make your own, all you need are a few household ingredients and about 10 minutes of good experimenting time.

YOU WILL NEED

- Vegetable oil
- Water
- Food coloring—any color will do
- Glitter or other pieces of small shiny paper
- A large glass jar with a lid

STEPS

1 POUR VEGETABLE OIL into a jar about a third of the way up.

2 SPRINKLE GLITTER or other shiny but small objects into the oil.

3 FILL THE JAR UP THE REST OF THE WAY with water. Be sure not to spray water into the jar with a strong stream. It's better to just pour it in from another glass, or the oil will break up into tiny bubbles, which will take a while to settle.

4 ADD THREE DROPS OF FOOD COLORING to the oil, glitter, and water mixture.

5 CLOSE THE JAR TIGHTLY with its lid.

6 TURN THE JAR OVER and watch the oil and glitter break up and float to the top. Shake the jar and flip it over and watch the oil and glitter float through the water. No matter how hard you shake, the two liquids will always separate out.

7 FOOD COLORING IS WATER-BASED, so will only color the water in your lava lamp. If you want to add another dimension—and a bit more color—to your lava lamp, find some oil paint and mix a little into your oil layer. The oil paint will not mix with the water layer for the same reason the water-based food coloring doesn't mix with the oil layer.

> # WARNING
>
> **Food coloring and oil paint will stain clothes, carpets, and furniture. Be careful not to spill any when you're shaking up your jar.**

This lava lamp works because oil and water do not mix together (scientists say they are "immiscible"). Not only is oil less dense than water, causing it to float on the surface (see page 28), but unlike some other liquids it doesn't dissolve in water. As a result, the oil will always float up to the top of the water, even after they've been mixed together, making cool patterns as it goes.

Real lava lamps use oil and liquid wax. They work without you having to shake or flip them because a light bulb in the lamp heats up the contents. The wax is carefully chosen because it is slightly more dense than oil when cool, but slightly less dense than oil when it warms up. When the light is switched on, it warms the cool, dense wax that's sunk to the bottom of the lamp. As it warms up, this wax gets less dense and floats towards the top in globules. When it reaches the top, it cools again because it's away from the lamp, and so becomes more dense again and sinks back down. Then it gets warm again, rises again, and so on.

This circular current of warming liquid is an example of convection, which occurs in all liquids and gases. Because the warm liquid circulates, cool liquid is constantly coming into contact with the heat element, meaning you can warm up an entire tank of water even if only the bottom of the tank is being heated.

DID YOU KNOW? Lava lamps only work at a particular temperature. If they get too warm, all the wax floats to the top and never cools enough to sink again. If they stay too cool, the wax never gets warm enough to float and just sits at the bottom of the lamp.

Fact Gathering

THE GREEK PHILOSOPHER SOCRATES ONCE SAID
"the only thing I know is that I know nothing." That
doesn't mean he was stupid. Lots of people think
Socrates was one of the smartest men who ever lived.
What he meant when he said that he knew nothing is
that, even though he had spent his whole life learning
as much as he possibly could, he could never know it
all. There's just too much stuff about life to know.

◆

After he made that statement, did Socrates close his
books and give up? Did he just stare out his window
without a curious thought in his mind for the rest of his
life? Nope. He understood that exploring means
knowing as much as possible about the world, in order
to make new discoveries. This chapter offers a few
important facts to help you on your explorations.

How a computer works

Computers are more than just calculators or equipment for playing video games. They're machines that organize and process all kinds of information. They take in data—from people, radio waves, sensors, and so on—process it, and output it in a form humans can understand. And they do it super-fast. Today, computers can be found in everything from cars to cameras, cell phones, and even toys. And for the explorer, they're an important means of finding out about the world.

All computers, no matter where they're found or what they do, have the same basic parts. They must all have programs to tell them what information to process, an operating system to tell them how to process it, a central processing unit to do the actual processing, and memory to store all the data they're working on.

The data itself comes from input devices. A mouse and a keyboard are both input devices—they allow you to give data to the computer to work on. Scientific instruments can also be input devices, passing their measurements to the computer. Devices such as screens, printers, or speakers are output devices, which tell us the results of the computer's calculations.

The program

Computers process data by acting out a set of instructions called a program. These instructions tell the computer exactly what to do with each bit of data. Each computer program has been written by humans in a computer language. A computer language is a way to write down complicated instructions in a logical, orderly way that computers can interpret. There are hundreds of different computer languages, that can be used to tell a computer to do anything from complex math to high-speed video games.

The operating system (OS)

Because a computer might have many different programs running at the same time, it needs one big program that can manage them all and decide how to share memory and processing power between them. This big program is called the operating system, or OS for short. An OS makes sure everything is running properly and efficiently.

The processor (CPU)

The central processing unit ("CPU" or "processor" for short) is the part of the computer that does all the hard work. This is a powerful microchip that can take in millions of bits of data every second, process them as instructed by the program, and output them. They pack an enormous amount of power into a very small space—some CPUs can fit on the end of your pinkie finger!

Memory

Once a CPU has done a calculation, it forgets everything—it has to move all the data right out again so it can process the next batch. For this reason, programs and data must be stored in a place where they can be retrieved by the CPU over and over. Storage is the function of computer memory.

Like humans, computers have both long-term and short-term memories. Long-term can be a magnetic disk inside the computer—called a "hard drive." Or it can be an optical disk like a CD or DVD that you can take in and out. Data can be stored on these even if the computer is turned off. Short-term memory can be accessed much more quickly, so it's used for work in progress on the computer. It's generally called "random access memory" or "RAM" for short, and only retains data while the computer is switched on. Without RAM, computers would have to take all their data from disks, which would be very slow.

DID YOU KNOW? One of the first digital computers ever invented was called the Electronic Numerical Integrator and Computer, or "ENIAC." It was designed to help make long range cannons more accurate during World War II. ENIAC weighed 28 tons—or as much as about 20 small cars—and cost nearly $500,000 to make. Compared to the most recent home computer processors, it was incredibly stupid. A home computer today can process 21.6 billion calculations a second. The ENIAC could manage 5,000 calculations a second, so long as one of its 17,468 vacuum tubes didn't blow up.

How a telephone works

Before telephones, telecommunication was limited to the telegraph, which sent an electronic current along a wire as a series of dots and dashes called Morse Code, which only trained telegraphers could understand. The alternative was writing letters and sending them by train or by boat, but these could take weeks to arrive, and might get lost along the way. The telephone made it possible for two people to talk as if they were in the same room together even though they were many miles apart.

Telephone technology is surprisingly simple, and hasn't changed that much since it was first invented in the 1870s. The human voice consists of a series of sound vibrations in the air. The telephone converts these vibrations to electric current by capturing them on a membrane. The current can be passed along a copper wire from one phone to the next. When the vibrations reach the connecting phone, another membrane converts them back into vibrations, at the same frequency as your voice, which travel through the air to your ear as sound.

Making it possible for any one phone to call so many other numbers is the really complicated part, but even that was solved relatively simply: by sending all the wires through a switchboard. In the old days, there were switchboard operators to match the correct wires together to make the connection. Now the connections are computerized, and switchboards are called "exchanges."

Cell-phone technology is different, of course, in that there are no wires connecting the phones to each other. In fact, they are actually more like radios. They transmit radio signals to nearby cell-phone towers, which act as exchanges to connect the radio signals to the receiving phones.

DID YOU KNOW? Most people think the Scots-American Alexander Graham Bell was the inventor of the telephone, but two other men—Antonio Meucci and Elisha Gray—discovered the same principle for transmitting sound electrically. Meucci actually had a patent on the idea 15 years before Bell, in 1860, but was unable to pay for its renewal in 1861. Bell and Gray battled in court for the patent in 1876 and Bell won.

Prisms

You've probably seen a thin ray of white light turned into a rainbow by a prism, but do you know how it works? Light is one of the most interesting things in the natural world, especially when you consider that it travels through space just like a baseball travels through the air when you throw it toward home plate. The big difference is that light is fast. Very fast.

Light is actually a form of radiation, like radio waves, which travels in waves with different wavelengths. Our eyes work by recognizing different wavelengths which our brains interpret as colors. White light is what we see when all the visible wavelengths hit our eyes at the same time. An object appears colorful when it absorbs some wavelengths of light but reflects others. A green shirt reflects the wavelengths our eyes recognize as green, but absorbs all the other wavelengths. A red shirt reflects only wavelengths we see as red, and so on. A black shirt absorbs every wavelength, so doesn't reflect anything for our eyes to pick up. A white shirt doesn't absorb any. (That's why your body will stay cooler in the summer if you wear white instead of black.)

Normally we can't see the different colored wavelengths in white light. At least not unless we use a prism. A prism is a transparent object with flat polished sides, and it can be made from glass, crystal, plastic, or even water. What makes a prism a prism is its ability to refract light inside itself—that means it 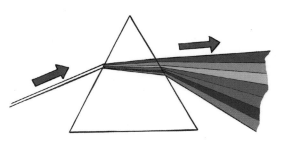 can break light up into its various wavelengths or colors. Light can move faster through air than it can through something solid like glass. When a ray of light hits a solid surface at an angle, it's slowed down. Different wavelengths of light travel with different energies, and the more energetic wavelengths are slowed less than the less energetic ones. This makes the different wavelengths move in slightly different directions, splitting the white light into rainbow colors.

Why the sky is blue

When we look into the sky, we're actually looking at the Earth's atmosphere, a layer of gases surrounding our planet. The atmosphere is a mixture: about 75 percent of it is nitrogen, 20 percent of it is oxygen, and the rest is mostly carbon dioxide with traces of a few other gases. Gravity holds these gases in place around the Earth like a big, clear blanket of air. And while they're wrapped around the planet, the gases also scatter light from the sun. The color of sky comes from the wavelengths of light that are scattered.

The sky appears blue because molecules of gas in the atmosphere scatter the blue wavelengths of light. Instead of coming directly to us from the Sun like other visible wavelengths, blue wavelengths are interfered with as they pass through the atmosphere and scatter off in all directions, so that the whole sky seems to us to be giving off blue wavelengths of light. This is called Rayleigh scattering, after John Rayleigh, the physicist who discovered it.

In the evening, when sunlight reaches us at a low angle as the sun sets, the light is broken up by another form of scattering called Mie scattering. In this case, dust particles in the lower atmosphere affect the light, creating orange, yellow, and red colors. Events that throw a lot of dust into the air—like sandstorms, forest fires, or volcanic eruptions—create the most spectacular colorful sunsets, because there is more scattering of the sun's rays as they come through the atmosphere.

DID YOU KNOW? There are some wavelengths of light that our eyes can't see. One such set of wavelengths is called infrared—these are the wavelengths emitted when heat radiates out from a warm object. Night goggles were invented to convert infrared wavelengths to colors we can see, so that we can pick out warm objects like animals or vehicle engines in the dark when there's no visible light to reflect off them.

The Solar System

A solar system is a collection of planets, asteroids, comets, and moons revolving in orbit around a star. Nobody knows how many solar systems there are to explore in the universe, but given there are hundreds of billions of stars in just our galaxy, the number is probably pretty high. Our solar system consists of eight planets and a load of moons, comets, and asteroids, all of them ripe for exploration by humans.

Compared to other stars in the universe, our Sun is actually only medium-sized. Even so, it would take 1.3 million Earths to fill the volume of the Sun. Like all stars, it consists of a vast ball of gases undergoing a nuclear reaction that gives off enormous quantities of energy. Scientists say that in four or five billion years—a very, very long time from now—the Sun will run out of nuclear fuel and will start to expand, burning up our planet and most of the solar system in the process.

The major planets in our solar system are Mercury, Venus, Earth, Mars, Jupiter, Saturn, Uranus, and Neptune. Mercury is the closest planet to the Sun, and Neptune is the one farthest away. For a long time scientists thought there were nine planets, but the ninth—Pluto—is so small it is now considered a "dwarf planet" instead.

Mercury is the smallest major planet in the solar system. It's covered with craters from comets crashing into it, because the planet is so small it doesn't have enough gravity to hold onto an atmosphere to protect it. Its temperatures range from 400°F (200°C) during the day to -300°F (-185°C) at night—the day side of the planet is roasted by being too close to the Sun, and the night side is frozen by being exposed to the coldness of space. Mercury would be a horrible place to live. It is named after the Roman god Mercury, who was the messenger of the gods.

Venus is the second planet from the Sun, and is nearer Earth than any other planet. Venus may be even more inhospitable than Mercury: the planet is covered in thousands of very active volcanoes, enormous lava fields, and hundreds of craters. The temperature gets up to 900°F (480°C) — hot enough to melt some metals — and the atmosphere is choked with poisonous clouds of sulfuric acid. Despite all this, Venus is named after the Roman goddess of love.

Our **Earth** was formed about 4.5 billion years ago, and is considered a rocky planet because it is made up of rocky layers with a molten core. Mercury, Venus, and Mars are also rocky planets. Earth is the only planet in the solar system that has liquid water on it (others have frozen water or ice), and scientists think that is why life was able to evolve here. Unlike Venus and Mercury, the Earth also has a moon.

Mars is the next planet out from the Sun. It is known as the Red Planet, because of the red color of its soil. Mars is a lot like Earth in many ways: it is a little colder and has a smaller gravity with a thinner atmosphere, but it may be possible for humans to live there one day. Its surface shows evidence of intense volcanic activity in the past, and possibly of running water. The highest known mountain in the solar system is Olympus Mons, an extinct volcano that rises 75,000 feet (23,000 m) above the surface of the planet — almost two and a half times as high as Mount Everest. There's also a massive canyon on the planet known as Valles Marineris that is 2,500 miles (4,000 km) long (about the width of the United States) and 4 miles (6.5 km) deep. For comparison, the Grand Canyon is only 1 mile (1.5 km) deep. Mars is named after the Roman god of war, and has two small moons named Phobos and Deimos (Greek for Fear and Dread, War's companions).

The rest of the planets in the solar system — Jupiter, Saturn, Uranus, and Neptune — are known as gas giants. They are made up mostly of gases and liquids rather than rock, with no solid surface, as far as we know. Gas giants can reach vast sizes, and their gravity often attracts several moons into orbit around them.

Jupiter is the first of the giant planets. It is made up mostly of hydrogen and helium in both gas and liquid forms. Some scientists think the whole planet is various forms of gas and some think it has a rocky core about 12 times the size of Earth. One of the most amazing features of Jupiter is its Great Red Spot — a massive storm in the atmosphere that has been going on for over 400 years. The storm is large enough to contain the Earth! Jupiter also has 60 moons, including Io (a planet of massive volcanos), Europa (an icy planet that some scientists hope has liquid water underneath its frozen surface), Ganymede (the largest moon in the Solar System), and Callisto. It is the biggest planet in the Solar System, and is named after the king of the Roman gods.

Saturn is the next giant planet out from the Sun. It is a gas planet surrounded by massive rings made up of hunks of ice and rock — you can see these from Earth with a telescope. Saturn is 95 times larger than Earth and has 31 moons. One of its moons — Titan — is so large it actually has its own atmosphere.

Uranus is another gas giant. It is made up mostly of icy methane gas, which gives it its blue appearance. Many scientists believe Uranus is still forming itself. The planet is so tilted on its axis that it sometimes looks like it's rolling through the universe like a giant bowling ball. It has 27 icy moons and a small ring system — similar to Saturn's, but nowhere near as large.

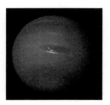

The last giant planet, and the planet farthest from the Sun, is **Neptune**. Like Uranus, Neptune has lots of icy methane in its atmosphere giving it a blue appearance. It also has a massive storm system in its atmosphere similar to Jupiter's Great Red Spot. The one on Neptune is called the Great Dark Spot. Neptune has 13 moons, the largest of which is Triton. Triton is an ice moon, but it has geysers on it that shoot ice 5 miles (8 km) high into the moon's atmosphere. Many scientists believe there is water beneath Triton's icy surface, which might possibly mean there could be life there.

Modeling the Solar System

———————————— ✦ ————————————

It's one thing to know that the Earth is 93 million miles (150 million km) from the Sun, and Neptune is 2.7 billion miles (4.3 billion km) from the Earth at its closest point. But what exactly would that look like? Here's a hint: it's a very, very long way. But with numbers that large, it's impossible to get a picture of it in your mind. Here's how to use a roll of toilet paper to help comprehend the enormous distances between the planets.

YOU WILL NEED

- A roll of toilet paper with 200 sheets per roll
- A room or hallway long enough to unroll the entire roll of toilet paper
- 10 different colored markers
- Clear tape

STEPS

1 STARTING AT ONE END OF THE ROOM OR HALLWAY, unroll the first sheet of toilet paper and tape it to the floor to hold it still.

2 MAKE A DOT ON THE PERFORATION between the first and second sheets (the dot should be about half the size of the end of a pencil). Label it "Sun." At the scale we're using to map out our paper solar system, this dot is an accurate representation of the size of the Sun. At this scale, the rest of the planets in the solar system would be too small to see, so we're going to mark them with "X."

3 NOW WE'RE GOING TO UNROLL THE ROLL OF TOILET PAPER on the floor and mark and label planets as they come up. Unroll 10 more sheets and mark "X"es on the paper in the following order: 2 sheets from the Sun is Mercury; 3.7 sheets from the Sun is Venus; 5.1 sheets from the Sun is Earth; and 7.7 sheets from the Sun is Mars.

4 NOW UNROLL ALL **200** SHEETS of the toilet paper.

5 JUPITER IS **26.4** SHEETS FROM THE SUN, Saturn is 48.4 sheets from the Sun, Uranus is 97.3 sheets away, and Neptune is at 152.4 sheets. Pluto, though it's technically not a planet, is exactly 200 sheets of toilet paper away.

DID YOU KNOW? There are lots of other things in our galaxy besides planets, including an asteroid belt (about 18 sheets from the Sun), comets, and moons. An unmanned spacecraft named *Voyager 2* was launched from Earth in 1977 to fly past and take pictures of as many planets in the Solar System as possible. In 1989, it flew past Neptune. Today it is more than 7.5 billion miles (12 billion km) from Earth—more than twice the distance that Pluto is from the Sun. *Voyager 2* still transmits weekly signals back to Earth. You can monitor its progress, and the progress of its sister spacecraft *Voyager 1*, even farther out in space, on the NASA website.

Now you've seen how huge the distances are between the planets, you can understand how difficult it is for human beings to travel to even our closest neighbors. Although Venus is the planet closest to us, its hostile atmosphere (see page 48) would make it pretty dangerous for any humans to visit. We're much more likely to travel to Mars, which is farther away but has a more similar atmosphere and temperature to our own planet.

Still, it's not an easy journey—it takes 18 months for a spacecraft from Earth to travel to Mars, and any humans on board would have to carry enough food, air, and water to last them for a minimum of three years, and enough fuel to get there and back. One way round the problem would be to equip a spacecraft with gardens to produce food and oxygen to keep the astronauts alive on their journey. This would need an enormous spaceship, which would be too big and fragile to lift off from Earth like a rocket or shuttle. Instead it might have to be constructed in orbit, by construction crews based on a space station, using materials shipped up from Earth in shuttles or unmanned rockets.

How wings work

For all the heartache, broken bones, and wacky experiments it took for explorers to figure out how to fly, the reason we can take to the air is really quite simple. And yes, it's all because of wings.

Wings work thanks to a basic physical rule called Bernoulli's principle. This says that air moving quickly over a surface creates a lower pressure than air moving slowly. If you can use this principle to create a lower pressure above an object than below it, the pressure will push that object upwards—this is called generating lift. By curving the top of the wings on an airplane and leaving the bottom of the wings flat, engineers cause the air flowing over the top of the wing to travel faster than the air under it. This causes a pressure difference that generates lift. This curved top and flat bottom wing design is called an airfoil.

Of course, to generate lift you have to have air moving over the wings, which means aircraft have to travel very fast. They use propellers or jet engines and a long runway to build up the required speed to take off. Helicopters work the same way, but spin the airfoils (blades on top) to move air over them rather than using a runway. The airfoils reduce the pressure above the helicopter and create lift.

The wings of birds also have this basic airfoil design. They don't, however, have jet packs to get them the speed they need to take off. That's why they have to flap their wings to generate uplift. Without flapping, their weight and the drag of their bodies would bring them back to earth. Some birds can glide once they get going with outstretched wings, using the same principle as an airplane. One bird, called a wandering albatross, can glide in the air without beating its wings for hours at a time. That's because it has the largest wingspan of any bird on the planet, reaching over 11 feet (3.3 m) from the tip of one wing to the tip of the other.

DID YOU KNOW? The largest plane ever built, at least in terms of wingspan, was made entirely out of wood. It was built in the 1940s by a millionaire called Howard Hughes, who named it the Spruce Goose. It was five stories tall and its wingspan was an enormous 319 feet and 11 inches (97.5 m). It was a flying boat, taking off and landing from the surface of the sea. The plane flew only once.

Metamorphosis

❧❧

The transition of a squiggly caterpillar into a magnificent butterfly—called metamorphosis—is nothing short of magical. When we see a caterpillar, we're actually seeing a butterfly in its larval stage—caterpillars hatch from eggs laid by butterflies. At this stage of their lives, they have only two goals: to eat as many leaves as they can, and to avoid getting eaten by birds or by other insects. The second goal is usually much harder than the first, although something not a lot of people know is that caterpillars actually can be pretty clever fighters. Some secrete a poisonous substance that makes them taste bad to birds, while others have fake eyes and the ability to inflate their heads to make themselves look like a threat, not a snack. Some even join up with ant colonies: the caterpillar gathers food for the ants and the ants in turn protect the caterpillar from predators.

Once the caterpillar has grown nice and fat, it finds a place to hide and creates a cocoon around itself. This is known as the pupal stage. It's here that the caterpillar's body changes, almost as though it's back in the egg. The straight body

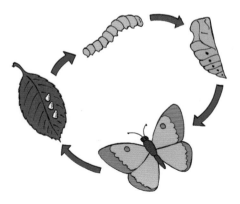

of the caterpillar turns into the segmented body of the butterfly, and the wings develop. After a few weeks, the caterpillar is fully grown into a butterfly, and it comes out of the cocoon. This stage is called the imago stage. The wings are crumpled up after growing inside the cocoon, and the butterfly must rest while it pumps them full of blood before it can fly.

You can watch the whole process for yourself by keeping caterpillars in an aquarium or large jar.

YOU WILL NEED ⚠

- A clean, empty fish tank or large jar
- Soil
- A water mister
- A pair of gardening shears
- Caterpillars
- Patience

STEPS

1 CLEAN OUT A FISH TANK OR LARGE GLASS JAR. If you're using a jar, punch holes in the lid to allow air in. Line the bottom with 2 inches (5 cm) soil from the garden. Add some sticks propped against the sides for the caterpillars to crawl on.

WARNING

Don't touch caterpillars, especially hairy ones. They certainly won't like it, and some of them can be poisonous to you as well.

2 GO FIND SOME CATERPILLARS! The best time to look is early summer, when you can find them on leaves of juicy plants. Don't touch the caterpillar when you find it, just cut the twig it's on off the plant and take it to your tank.

3 KEEP THE CATERPILLAR IN YOUR TANK, giving it a fresh supply of leaves every day from the plant you found it on. If you spot mold growing on the soil, carefully scrape it out, throw it away, and scatter fresh soil in place.

4 KEEP THE CONTAINER OUT OF DIRECT SUNLIGHT, so it doesn't get too hot, and give it a little misting of water if it's drying out.

5 AFTER A FEW WEEKS, your caterpillar will wrap itself in a cocoon. Keep watching, and it'll emerge as a butterfly. You should release the butterfly when it hatches so it can lay more caterpillar eggs and start the cycle again.

DID YOU KNOW? The cocoons of the silk moth caterpillar are made from soft, very strong fibers that humans use to make silk clothing.

Why leaves change color

❖

The beautiful colors of fall are impressive, but leaves don't change colors for our benefit. Everything in nature happens for a reason, and colorful leaves are no different. Leaves change colors because the trees are trying to save energy before the long cold winter.

First of all, leaves are green because they contain a substance called chlorophyll. Plants don't eat, they make all their food inside their leaves by absorbing sunlight to convert carbon dioxide and water into sugars—a process known as photosynthesis. The chlorophyll in the leaves is what plants use to capture sunlight. A tree spends a lot of its energy making more chlorophyll for its leaves so it can continue to grow. During the winter, though, when daylight hours aren't as long as they are in the summer and there's less sunlight to make energy from, trees will stop making chlorophyll and hibernate to conserve their energy for the spring. When the tree stops replenishing chlorophyll, the green color goes out of the leaves.

After the green is gone, other colors in the leaves start to show through. The yellow-brown colors come from chemicals already in the leaf that help with photosynthesis. The yellow is always there—we just can't see it the rest of the time because the green chlorophyll usually covers it up. The red and purple colors you see on some trees come from other chemicals, which are used to break down sugars in the leaf—the tree needs to take as much nourishment as it can from the leaves before dropping them.

Building a leaf press

If want to preserve some especially colorful leaves, so they don't go brown and boring, you can build a press.

YOU WILL NEED
- Colorful leaves
- 2 pieces of plywood at least 6 inches (15 cm) on each side
- 2 clamps (or a large pile of heavy books)
- Sheets of tissue paper

STEPS:

1 START WITH ONE OF THE BOARDS: lay it flat on a table and cover it with three or four layers of tissue paper. Make sure there are no wrinkles or creases in the paper—you want as smooth a layer as possible.

2 CHOOSE YOUR FAVORITE LEAVES and lay them on the tissue paper. Leave at least a ½-inch (1.2-cm) gap between neighboring leaves.

3 COVER THE LEAVES with another three or four layers of tissue paper. Make sure to keep it smooth again. Put the other board on top.

4 FINALLY, EITHER SCREW CLAMPS TIGHTLY at each end of the boards, or pile plenty of heavy books or even bricks on top.

5 LEAVE THE WHOLE SET-UP IN A COOL, DRY PLACE, and the moisture will be squeezed out of the leaves and drawn into the tissue paper. After a few weeks, you will be left with dried out, flattened leaves, with the fall colors preserved.

DID YOU KNOW? The world's largest leaves come from the Raffia palm. They can grow up to 80 feet (25 m) long!

Measuring a tree's age

❖

Used to be the only way to tell a tree's age was to cut down the tree. Each concentric ring found on the stump of a tree accounts for one year of its life. That's because each year a new layer of wood grows around a tree's trunk, branches, and roots.

Telling the age of a tree by counting its concentric rings is not foolproof, though. The heartwood of some of the oldest trees (the wood at its very center) sometimes decays, leaving a big gap in years. Besides, there are times when scientists want to tell the age of a tree without ending its life. To do that they've discovered a fast method of guessing a tree's age that doesn't involve a saw.

YOU WILL NEED
- A flexible tape measure
- A tree

STEPS

1 MEASURE THE DISTANCE around the tree at about 5 feet (1.5 m) off the ground.

2 IF THE TREE IS IN A DENSE FOREST and surrounded by other trees, it's been growing slowly because it's been competing with other trees for sunlight. These trees usually have long straight trunks without many side branches. In this case, about every ½ inch (1.2 cm) of girth equals one year of age.

3 IF THE TREE IS STANDING ALONE with lots of side branches and a clear path to sunlight, that means it's had an easy life and has grown fast. In this case, about every inch (2.5 cm) of girth equals one year of life.

DID YOU KNOW? The oldest known tree is a bristlecone pine named Methuselah. It is over 4,723 years old—that means it seeded about the time the Pyramids were built.

Fingerprints

✦✦✦

Human skin is always slightly greasy to help it keep supple and prevent cracking. When you touch a smooth surface like metal or glass, you leave a little of this grease behind in the shape of your fingerprint. Police around the world have been perfecting techniques for collecting and identifying these prints for over 100 years. In fact, the first fingerprint bureau opened at a police headquarters in India in 1897. Today, finding fingerprints is still a useful way to get the bad guys, supported by more modern forensic techniques like DNA matching.

Fingerprints are the ridges on your fingertips, that were formed into a unique pattern before you were even born. The ridges loop, arch, whirl, and branch off, and most also have dots. Every person's fingerprints are permanent: they do not change as you get older (unlike your nose and ears, which keep growing). They're also completely unique — not even identical twins have the same fingerprints.

In the old days, before computers, matching a fingerprint found at a crime scene took a long time, because the police had to compare them all by eye with every other print on their records. Sometimes mistakes were made and the wrong person went to jail. Today, fingerprint matching is still challenging, but advances in technology have made it much more efficient. Computers can now electronically match prints in a very short amount of time. The FBI has over 70 million fingerprints stored on its computers.

The first ever criminal to be caught thanks to a fingerprint was an Argentinian woman named Fransisca Rojas. Her bloody print was found at the scene of a murder in 1892, by a policeman named Juan Vucetich, a pioneer in fingerprint identification.

Here's how to collect and identify your own fingerprints, for practice:

YOU WILL NEED:

- An ink pad
- A sheet of white paper
- A sheet of black paper
- A smooth glass surface
- A soft paintbrush with very fine hairs
- Very fine flour
- Clear sticky tape

STEPS:

1 ROLL A FINGER ACROSS A GLASS SURFACE to leave your distinctive print behind.

2 CREATE A REFERENCE by rolling the same finger on an ink pad, then on the white paper. This will give your fingerprint as a sample.

3 WITH THE PAINTBRUSH, gently dust flour across the place on the glass where you left your print. The flour will stick to the grease your finger left behind.

4 STICK A STRIP OF TAPE across the dusted print and carefully lift it off again. It should bring the dust outline of your print with it.

5 STICK THE TAPE TO THE BLACK PAPER and compare it with your sample print. You should be able to see a white outline with an identical pattern!

Fingerprints aren't just used to catch criminals — more and more technology is being developed to use them for identification and security in everyday life. Computers that can recognize prints can be attached to locks, so that only people with the correct fingerprints can get through. Or they can be connected to bank systems to confirm someone's identity when they withdraw money.

DID YOU KNOW? Humans aren't the only animals to have fingerprints. Other primates, including gorillas and chimpanzees, also have them. More surprisingly, so do koala bears!

Plaster casts

❦❦

Plaster casts are one way naturalists and other explorers gather facts. They can record and study fossils, footprints, leaves, bones, and other things found on their adventures by mixing up a simple recipe wherever they are. It's a lot easier than digging the whole thing out and dragging it back to the lab!

If you're interested in nature, you can use plaster of paris to make a permanent record of any interesting tracks you find. If you're lucky enough to dig up a fossil (see page 64), you can use the same technique to make copies for your friends. Or, if you're on the trail of a dangerous criminal, you can take plaster casts of their footprints as evidence.

YOU WILL NEED

- An animal footprint
- Water
- Dry plaster of paris
- A plastic cup
- Putty (optional)

STEPS

1 THE NEXT TIME YOU HIT THE TRAIL to discover nature, look for some animal footprints. If you can't find an animal print, practice by making a print with your own foot.

2 MIX 2 CUPS (500 ML) OF WATER with 3 cups (750 ml) of plaster of paris, adding the water a little at a time as you stir so you don't get lumps.

3 POUR THE LIQUID PLASTER mix right into the print until it overflows a little at the top.

③

4 LEAVE THE PLASTER TO DRY for an hour, then pull it up, wash off the soil, and you'll have an exact match of the print you found!

5 IF YOU WANT TO MAKE A CAST of an interesting leaf or shell that you've found, get a jar or two of putty, roll it out into a thick pancake, and then press your discovery into it. Once you get a good impression, mix up your plaster and pour it into the putty as you would have into the soil on the trail.

WARNING

Plaster of paris undergoes a chemical reaction with water as it hardens, which gives out a lot of heat. Never attempt to make plaster casts of your hands or feet, or any other body part, as you can suffer severe burns inside the plaster as it sets.

6 IF YOU WANT TO CREATE A THREE-DIMENSIONAL CAST of a shell or bone, make two pancakes of putty. Push half the object into one pancake, then take the second pancake and push it down on top to cover the other half of the object. When you're sure you have a good imprint, remove the top pancake carefully and set it down. Then remove the shell or bone from the first pancake. Mix up your plaster and pour it into each half, taking care to make sure the level of plaster is flush with the top of the mold and that it doesn't overflow. After it dries, you can glue the two halves together to make a permanent plaster copy of your discovery.

When the Roman town of Pompeii, in Italy, was buried by a volcanic eruption in 79 AD, people trapped in the path of the eruption were buried under ash. Over the years the ash hardened and the bodies rotted away, leaving a hollow imprint of the buried people under the ground. Modern archelogists have discovered these hollows and use plaster casts to make copies of them, showing us exactly how these people looked when they were buried.

DID YOU KNOW? Plaster of paris is named after the city of Paris, in France, because that's where one of the ingredients — a chemical called gypsum — was quarried.

Archeology

An important area of fact gathering is finding out about the past. Historians do this by looking at old records and manuscripts. Archeologists do this by getting out there and digging around to find old stuff that's been buried for hundreds, thousands, or even millions of years. The evidence they find can tell us anything from exactly what happened on a particular battlefield, to what life was like for our early ancestors, and even what the world looked like before humans came on the scene, in the days when dinosaurs ruled the earth.

Of course, evidence from so long ago is often hard to find. Soft materials like flesh, wood, and clothing all rot away; earthquakes can cause buildings to collapse; and water, wind, and weather can cover everything over and bury it underground. What makes archeologists different from ordinary people with spades and a sense of curiosity, is that archeologists have developed extensive techniques to find interesting sites, work out exactly where to dig, and extract the maximum information about the past from what they find.

Finding the site

Of course, archeologists don't just dig around any old place. They do careful research to work out where's the best place to look for whatever bits of history they're interested in. If you're looking for fossils, the type of rock is important: fossils only occur in sedimentary rocks, that is rocks made from mud layers laid down millions of years ago.

For more recent history, they often go back to historical records, looking at old documents, local stories, or even myths and legends recording the sites of ancient cities, temples, or battlefields. Or they look for interesting formations above ground: burial mounds and defensive earthworks leave unusual ridges and hummocks on the landscape, and buried foundations can cause dry patches in the soil above them creating "shadows" in any grass or crops growing on top.

The Tomb of King Tutankhamun

Sometimes it's obvious where to look: archeologists interested in Ancient Egypt have known for centuries that the Pyramids were a good place to start looking. If anything, the problem is that they were too obvious, and grave-robbers and souvenir-seekers had already broken into and looted many tombs. The Valley of the Kings at Luxor, farther up the Nile, is the burial site of many Egyptian pharoahs, but by the 1920s it was so well known and excavated that most people believed there was nothing left to find.

One man, however, called Howard Carter, had become obsessed with a little-known pharoah called Tutankhamun, and was convinced that his tomb lay undiscovered somewhere in the Valley. In 1922, he found it—the only undisturbed pharoah's tomb ever found, and one of the richest archeological finds in history. The four rooms contained thousands of precious items, from pots of perfume, to entire chariots, gold plate, statues, and of course the sarcophagus containing the mummified body of Tutankhamun.

DID YOU KNOW? Although the discovery made them both famous, both Carter and his employer, Lord Carnarvon, died in mysterious circumstances some years after the discovery of the tomb. Legends persist that they suffered an ancient curse placed upon anybody who disturbed Tutankhamun's ancient resting place.

Geophysics

Once a good site has been identified, archeologists want to get some idea what's under the ground before they start the hard work of digging trenches. Howard Carter took 15 years to find Tutankhamun's tomb, even though he knew roughly where to look. Archeologists nowadays use scientific instruments to get a picture of what's down there. The science is called "geophysics," and it uses these three main techniques:

Electrical resistance: By measuring how well the ground conducts electricity, geophysicists can identify buried stone foundations (which block electrical currents), or areas of organic or burnt matter (which conduct a little better than plain soil).

Magnetism: The Earth's natural magnetic field can be disrupted by buried metal, or by the remains of earthworks or foundations. Very sensitive measurements are taken to plot these disruptions and use them to build up a picture of what might be buried beneath the soil.

Ground-penetrating radar (GPR): Like the radar used by aircraft and ships, GPR works by sending out radio waves and seeing what bounces back. Dense areas underground, like packed earth or stone, will bounce back a stronger signal than soil.

In each case, the scientists survey an area and use computers to generate maps. Sometimes these maps can show the exact layout of a building's foundations buried underground. Other times, they just show up areas that might be interesting, so the archeologists can get digging and see what's down there.

Excavation

Once a site has been found, archeologists must carefully excavate the area to find out as much as they can. Digging up ancient artifacts is always exciting, but archeologists can gain as much information from where an object was found as from the object itself. For example, the deeper an object is buried, the older it's likely to be. If it was found in an area with bits of old bone, shell, and other trash, it was probably thrown away, but if it was carefully wrapped up and placed in a hidey-hole it was probably hidden for safe-keeping.

Even the soil surrounding a find might carry information, as it may contain fragments of decayed cloth, or evidence of old ashes or rotted food. Archeologists are trained to pick out the tiniest details, even down to grains and seeds, and use them to identify how people lived, what they wore and ate, how they worshipped, and how they treated their dead.

Dinosaur bones

The study of dinosaur bones is part of paleontology, which is the study of fossils. Fossils are the remains of animals and plants from millions of years ago which are preserved by being buried in mud. The layers of mud are compressed by the weight of more mud settling on top, which gradually turns them into rock. The remains undergo a process called "permineralization," which preserves an impression of them in stone. If the conditions are right, anything from huge dinosaur bones, to plants, tiny plankton, and even footprints can become fossilized.

Some of these fossils are revealed by erosion removing the top layers of soil and rock so that the bones become visible. When archeologists know that an area is likely to contain fossils, they can use geophysics to find their position underground.

Perhaps the most famous fossil discoveries are, of course, the dinosaurs—giant lizards that were the largest and most common animals on Earth from about 230 million years ago until about 65 million years ago. They ranged from massive herbivores called sauropods—the largest of which, *Supersaurus*, might have been as much as 130 feet (40 m) from head to tail—to carnivores like the *Tyrannosaurus rex*, and bird-like creatures like *Archaeopteryx*.

> ## WARNING
>
> **Because every piece of evidence is important, information can be easily destroyed by amateur digging. While it's fun to see what you can unearth in your back yard, you shouldn't try excavating at real archeological sites in case you damage precious evidence.**

DID YOU KNOW? The badlands of Colorado and Utah have some of the richest deposits of dinosaur fossils anywhere in the world. There's even a town in Colorado called Dinosaur in their honor.

The Terracotta Army

In 1974, farmers digging a well near Mount Lishan in central China discovered a number of life-sized terracotta models of soldiers. Archeologists were quickly called in, and continuing excavations have unearthed more than 7,000 pottery warriors, horses, and chariots, with all the weapons and equipment for an army. Careful analysis of the statues and equipment found along with them has connected them to the tomb of Qin Shi Huangdi, the first Emperor of China, which is known to lie nearby. The tomb itself is believed to contain even greater wonders, but archeologists are concerned that it is too fragile to withstand excavation. As a result, it will remain untouched until the right techniques have been developed.

Latitude and longitude

Latitude and longitude is a system for describing any position in the world using coordinates. It works by overlaying the Earth with a grid of imaginary lines running north-south and east-west.

The north-south lines run from the North to the South Pole. The system was invented in England, so the central north-south line (known as the Prime Meridian or Greenwich Meridian) runs through the Royal Greenwich Observatory in London. The east-west lines run in bands around the Earth, with the central band being the Equator right around the middle.

When a sailor refers to latitude, that means the distance north or south of the Equator, while longitude is the distance east or west of the Prime Meridian. These positions are usually referred to in degrees, since they were originally calculated by their angle from the center of the Earth. The Equator is 0° latitude, the North Pole is 90° north and the South Pole is 90° south. The Prime Meridian is 0° longitude. East of the Prime Meridian, the number increases up to +180° longitude. When you go west of the Prime Meridian you must state longitude in negative terms, to -180°. New York is located at 40.47° N (latitude) by -73.58° (longitude). Hong Kong is 22.18° N by 114.10°. London is 59.29° N by 0° (remember the city sits directly on the Prime Meridian).

Latitude has always been easy to figure out because a seasoned sailor could always use the angle of the Sun, Moon, or North Star to judge their distance from the Equator. Longitude was the tricky part. At first the only way to determine longitude was to mark your location in relation to a body of land—a process known as dead reckoning—but this didn't work once you were out of sight of land. In 1781, sailors worked out how to use a clock to calculate longitude, by measuring the difference in time-zone between their starting point and their position on the sea. The difference in time between noon shown on the clock, and noon shown by the sun, told them how far round the Earth they had sailed.

Roman numerals

Figuring out ways to record numbers has interested humans for at least 30,000 years. Scientists discovered bones in Southern Africa from that period with tally marks on them — little slashes that someone may have used to count how many animals they'd killed, or how many days passed.

By the time of the Romans, things were more sophisticated. The Roman system of numerals (numbers) was used across Europe for a thousand years before they were replaced in the Middle Ages by the Arabic system of numbers we use today. We still use Roman numerals, although mostly for stylistic reasons rather than actual counting. If you've ever wondered how to decipher them, here's how.

Roman numerals use seven basic symbols. By combining them, the Romans could express any number all the way to infinity — starting, of course, with one. The seven symbols are:

I = One
V = Five
X = Ten
L = Fifty
C = One hundred
D = Five hundred
M = One thousand

The basic method for counting with Roman numerals is to add the symbols together to make a number:

I = One
II = Two
III = Three

However, when you're one away from using a new symbol (V) it changes a bit. IV means four—it basically says, "We are one away from five." Once you reach five, then you start counting with V as the first symbol, so:

V = Five
VI = Six
VII = Seven
VIII = Eight

But once you've almost reached 10 (X) you do the same as you did for five (V).

IX = Nine (one away from 10)
XI = 11
XII = 12
XIII = 13
XIV = 14
XV = 15, and so on.

Nineteen is XIX (10 plus one-away-from-10, or 10 plus 9). Twenty is XX and 30 is XXX, but 40 is XL (ten away from 50), so 42 is XLII (10 away from 50, plus two). Sixty is LX, 70 is LXX, and so on. Ninety would be XC (10 away from 100). Four hundred would be CD, 600 would be DC, and 900 would be CM. And so on. Essentially, if a smaller numeral is to the left of a larger number, you should subtract that numeral from the larger number. If it is to the right, you should add it. But if you try to line them up in columns to do sums, you can see you quickly get into problems. There is no zero in Roman numerals, so it's very hard to use them for math.

DID YOU KNOW? Latin numerals were replaced with Arabic numerals—the numbers we use today—around the 12th century AD. Europeans began calling the numerals "Arabic" because they came to Europe from the Middle East. However, the numerals actually originated with cultures located in modern India.

How an engine works

Boys of all ages find engines fascinating. Something about the noise and power that they can create gets us interested. But how do they work? Well, at heart they're not as complicted as you might think. Engines are basically just machines for turning fuel into energy. In a generator, the energy is converted to electricity. In a car, the energy is used to move the car and whatever's in it along the road.

The engines in most motor vehicles are internal combustion engines—that is, engines that burn their fuel inside the machine, not outside like an old-fashioned steam engine. They do this by burning fuel in cylinders. A cylinder is a sealed chamber with a spark plug fixed into the top, and a piston that makes an airtight seal at the bottom. The piston can move up and down inside the cylinder to change the space inside it. Each cylinder also has two valves, one to let fuel in, and one to let the exhaust out.

Car engines are usually four-stroke engines, which means they extract energy from fuel in a cycle made up of four stages: injection, compression, combustion, and exhaust. Here's an outline of how they work:

A four-stroke engine

1 IN THE INJECTION STAGE, the liquid fuel is squirted through one of the valves and into the cylinder. The squirting is important because it mixes the fuel with air, helping it to burn more energetically. In this stage, the piston is moving down to help draw the fuel into the chamber.

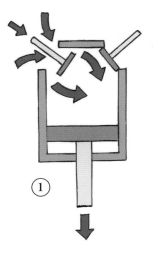

2 IN THE <u>COMPRESSION</u> STAGE, both valves seal shut and the piston rises in the cylinder, squeezing the fuel up into a small space near the spark plug at the top of the cylinder.

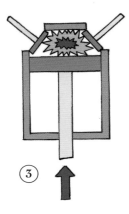

3 NOW COMES THE <u>IGNITION</u> STAGE: the compressed air and fuel mixture is ignited by the spark plug. Because of the pressure caused in the compression stage, the fuel burns in a mini-explosion, creating a lot of hot gas that forces the piston back down to the bottom of the cylinder. The engine converts this driving force into torque that turns the wheels of the car.

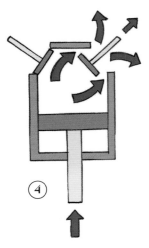

4 THE FINAL PHASE IS <u>EXHAUST</u>, where the hot waste gases, now that they've done their job, are allowed to exit the cylinder through the other valve. The piston rises up to help push them out. They come out the tail pipe. Once they're gone, the process can start all over again with new fuel coming in through the injection valve.

Most engines have several cylinders, all going through the same cycle to drive the car forward. The more cylinders you have and the bigger they are, the more powerful your engine will be.

Other elements of the engine include the radiator, which circulates water around the cylinders to prevent them from getting too hot. There's also an oil reservoir that allows grease to circulate round the moving parts and stop them from rusting up. A carburetor mixes the fuel with air before it is injected into the chamber, to ensure that the right proportions are there for the best combustion. The battery provides electricity to the spark plugs, as well as the headlights, windshield wipers, stereo, and anything else in the car that runs on electricity. The battery recharges by taking some of the energy from the engine as it's running, so that the car can start next time you need to drive.

Other types of engines

There are plenty of other types of engines, although the four-stroke is the most common. Big cars and trucks often use diesel engines, which work in a similar way but burn diesel fuel instead of gasoline, and don't use spark plugs. Instead, they compress air to very high pressures inside the cylinder before allowing it into contact with the fuel. The air heats up as it's squeezed into a small space, and that heat is what sets the fuel burning. Diesel engines produce more energy than gasoline engines from the same amount of fuel, but they're also heavier. This makes them more efficient than gasoline for larger machines like trucks, but less efficient for smaller ones like sports cars.

Two-stroke engines are found on smaller machines, like lawnmowers or motor-scooters. In these engines, the engine draws in new fuel, compresses it, and pushes out exhaust gas all in the same movement, before igniting the fuel. Because it does everything at once, some of the fuel tends to escape with the exhaust, making these engines less efficient and more polluting than four-stroke engines.

Airplanes often use jet engines. These are essentially tubes filled with spinning blades, which draw air in at the front as they spin and compress it inside the tube. The compressed air is mixed with fuel and ignited, and the burning fuel creates hot gas at high pressure like in a four-stroke engine. The high-pressure gas is allowed to escape at the back of the tube, and it comes out moving pretty fast. The jet of exhaust at the back is what pushes the airplane along. (Airplanes with propellors, however, usually have a four-stroke to turn the propellor.)

Rocket engines work in a similar way to jet engines — burning fuel under pressure to create a jet of hot gas that launches the rocket upward. But rockets don't burn fuel in air — instead they carry oxygen along with them and mix it with fuel inside the rocket. Burning is a chemical reaction between oxygen and fuel, so using pure oxygen rather than air (which is only about 20 percent oxygen) helps the fuel burn more powerfully.

DID YOU KNOW? The power produced by an engine is often measured in horsepower. In 1782, an engineer called James Watt came up with the term when he was designing engines for a lifting mechanism at a coal mine. Ponies were used to drive the machinery before the engines were installed, so Watt measured the power of his engines by how many ponies'-worth of work they could do.

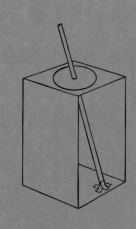

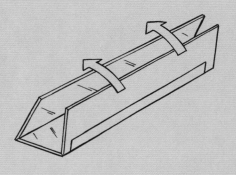

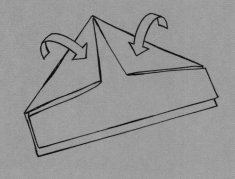

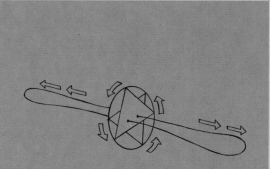

Chapter Three

Constructing

SOMETIMES THE BEST THING TO EXPLORE
is our own ability to create and build. When we
build things, not only do we end up with lots of cool
stuff, but we get to see what kind of construction
skills are hiding inside of us. Plus, building things
yourself is a great way to discover how they work.

◆

Ever wonder how a hovercraft can travel on both
water and land? Make your own and find out. How
do you tell time by the sun? Build a sundial and see.
This chapter will help you explore your power to
make something new.

A hovercraft

❖

Hovercrafts are floating ships that can travel over both land and water, making them very useful in swamps and other unreliable terrain. But how do they work? Unfortunately, the secret has nothing to do with anti-gravity. Instead they simply use huge fans to create an air cushion between themselves and the land or water underneath, so that they can glide over the top of any surface.

Because they hardly touch the terrain they're traveling over, hovercraft experience very little friction—the force that slows down two surfaces moving against each other. This means that they can reach impressive speeds: the world record is 85 mph (137 kmph). But for the same reason they can be pretty hard to steer, skidding round corners, especially at high speeds. And they don't have any brakes. Hoevercraft stop by letting down the cushion of air so the craft comes to rest. That's one reason why you don't see a lot of hovercraft out on the roads.

Nevertheless, enthusiasts around the world build and race small hovercraft, mostly built to hold just one person. The races take place over a variety of terrain and half the challenge is keeping your ride on the course.

To see how this works, try simulating a real hovercraft with a tabletop model. All you need are a few household items. This is a nice easy project to get you started, and shouldn't take you more than 10 minutes once the glue has dried.

YOU WILL NEED

- An old CD
- A pull-up water-bottle lid
- Glue

- A balloon
- A table top

STEPS

1 GLUE THE WATER BOTTLE LID over the center hole of the old CD, and let it sit until it's dry—this might take a few hours, so leave it overnight. Make sure the glue goes all the way round the bottle lid, so that air can't escape at the edges.

2 **WHEN THE GLUE HAS DRIED,** pull up the bottle lid as if you're going to take a drink of water.

3 **BLOW UP THE BALLOON ALL THE WAY** and pinch the neck to prevent air from getting out. (Don't tie it off, though, since you're going to want to let the air out any moment.)

4 **WHILE STILL HOLDING THE BALLOON CLOSED,** pull the rim of the balloon neck over the bottle top so it makes a good seal. Then set the CD down on a flat surface—a table top or polished floor works great.

5 **LET GO OF THE BALLOON** so the air can come out through the bottle top. The CD should lift off the table! Give it a gentle push and watch it glide.

6 **JUST LIKE A REAL HOVERCRAFT,** a cushion of air is being forced under the CD (from the pressure inside the balloon) that allows it to levitate off the ground. Because the bottom of the CD is pushed away from the surface of the table, it can glide along for quite a distance, at least until the air in the balloon runs out.

⑤

7 **HOWEVER, UNLIKE A REAL HOVERCRAFT,** your model doesn't have a skirt to hold the air in and maintain the high pressure. This means it runs down a lot quicker, and it's also less stable where the surface it's traveling over isn't smooth and firm. You can try getting it to work on a flat pool of water, but you might well find your CD just flips over.

DID YOU KNOW? The world's largest passenger hovercraft was built by the British to cross the English Channel to France. It was 185 feet (56 m) long, weighed 350 tons, and could carry 418 passengers and 60 cars!

A compass

❖❖

Invented in China over 1,000 years ago, compasses use the Earth's magnetic field to tell you which way is north. Movement of lava beneath the Earth's crust creates a very weak magnetic field running between the planet's North and South Poles. A very light magnetic needle, if it's allowed to swing freely, will align itself with this field, because the poles on magnets attract and repel each other. This means the needle will always swing round to point north, no matter how you turn it, and that can help you find your way if your quest for discovery ever takes you a little too far from the lab.

Unfortunately, there are times we forget to pack a real compass. No worries—you can make one. Fortunately, the Earth's magnetic field is strong enough to attract magnetized sewing needles or paper clips, if they're given freedom to spin by being floated on water. Here's how to set up your own so you can always tell which way is north:

YOU WILL NEED

- A magnet
- A plastic container to hold water
- Water
- A leaf or large blade of grass
- A small piece of metal, like a needle, paperclip, or small nail

STEPS

1 RUN THE MAGNET SLOWLY over the needle about 10 times, in the same direction each time. This will make the needle magnetic enough to act as a compass.

2 IF YOU DON'T HAVE A MAGNET you can still magnetize your needle or paper clip using static electricity. You can use material from a nylon raincoat or fleece jacket to build up the charge. Simply stroke the needle in the same direction with the material you have on hand. Do this at least 50 times.

3 FILL A PLASTIC CONTAINER with water, and gently place a leaf or large blade of grass so it floats on top in the center of the container.

4 CAREFULLY PLACE THE MAGNETIZED NEEDLE on top of the floating leaf or grass, so it floats freely on the surface of the water.

5 WATCH AS THE NEEDLE TURNS to point itself towards the North Pole.

WARNING

This method won't work if you use a bowl made from metal to hold the water. The magnetized needle will be attracted to the metal bowl insead of swinging freely to point north.

6 TRY TO TEST YOUR HOMEMADE COMPASS in a place that's sheltered from the wind. Earth's magnetic poles might be strong enough to attract a magnetized needle but that's not saying much. A breeze, even a gentle one, can easily push your leaf off course.

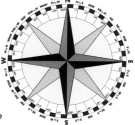

7 OF COURSE, THIS WILL ONLY SHOW YOU a line between north and south. You need some other clues to work out which is which. The sun is one clue: in the northern hemisphere, the sun will always be in the southern half of the sky, on the eastern side in the morning and the western side in the evening. In the southern hemisphere, the sun will always be on the northern side of the sky.

DID YOU KNOW? You've heard of north, south, east, and west, but did you know old-time sailors divided the compass into 32 points? There are seven points between north and east: northeast is halfway between the two; north-northeast is halfway between north and northeast; north-by-east is halfway between north-northeast; and so on. A diagram showing all 32 points is called a "compass rose." Modern compasses are divided into 360 degrees, for even more accurate measurements.

A sundial

Sundials are the world's oldest clocks—they work on the simple principle that the sun is always in the same direction at noon: directly south in the northern hemisphere, and directly north in the southern hemisphere. (At noon on the Equator, in case you were wondering, the sun is always directly overhead.) By making your own sundial, you can tell time using the sun and the shadows it creates. Constructing the device takes about 10 minutes, but marking the clock face takes several hours—from 9 AM to 3 PM—as the sun moves across the sky.

YOU WILL NEED

- A shoebox
- A screwdriver
- A straight stick—bamboo works well
- Masking tape
- A black marker
- A compass
- A full sunny day

STEPS

1 TURN THE SHOEBOX ON ITS END. Draw a circle in the middle of one end.

2 USING A SCREWDRIVER, poke a hole in the middle of the circle. Then poke a hole in the bottom of the shoebox below the first hole, but a little further back.

3 PUSH YOUR STICK THROUGH THE FIRST HOLE and angle it back toward the end of the shoebox. Push the tip of the stick through the second hole you made and tape it in place. Your stick should now be firmly held so it pokes up at an angle out of the circle on the top of the box.

4 TAKE YOUR SUNDIAL OUTSIDE and place it on a flat surface out in the open where it won't be disturbed. If you need to steady it against the wind, you can

put a large stone or brick in the bottom of the shoebox.

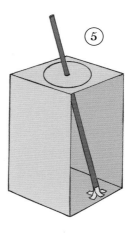

5 USE A COMPASS TO FIND NORTH, and point the stick in that direction if you're in the northern hemisphere, or south if you're in the southern hemisphere. The stick should throw a good, clear shadow across the circle you drew.

6 AT EXACTLY 9 AM, draw a line marking the position of the shadow of the stick on the circle you drew in step 1. Mark it with a straight line and label it 9 AM.

7 EACH HOUR AFTER THAT, REVISIT YOUR SUNDIAL and mark the new location of the shadow with 10 AM, 11 AM, 12 noon, 1 PM, 2 PM and 3 PM. Your sundial is now ready to tell the time. If you want your sundial to work before 9 AM, you have to get up early and mark the shadow exactly on the hour. If you want it to work later, keep marking the shadow on the hour until the sun goes down.

8 ANY TIME YOU WANT TO USE THE SUNDIAL, take it outside and use your compass to point the stick in the right direction, as you did in step 5. Then see where the shadow falls in relation to the lines you've already drawn.

9 REMEMBER THAT IF YOUR LOCAL TIME CHANGES by an hour from winter into summer, your sundial will only be correct for the time of year when you set it up.

DID YOU KNOW? Obelisks—giant, pointed stone pillars—were often used in Ancient Egyptian architecture, and some archaeologists believe they were used as large public sundials or clocks so that people could keep their schedules. The Washington Monument in Washington DC is an obelisk— although it's too big to use it to tell the time.

Bottle music

✦

Many years ago, explorers discovered that people of ancient civilizations thought music was the language of the spirits, and that by making music you were talking to the other world. If you want to talk to the other world, or just play some tunes, one good way to make a musical instrument at home—without having to carve a violin out of a hunk of mahogany—is to tap on a few bottles.

Explorers found out that, if you fill bottles with different levels of water, you'll get different notes when you tap them. That's because when you tap a bottle with a stick you are causing the bottle to vibrate—the vibrations transmit into the air and produce a sound. Water inside a bottle dampens these vibrations. The less water in the bottle, the faster the glass will vibrate, while more water will produce slower vibrations. Fast vibrations in the air produce a high-pitched note, and slower vibrations produce a lower pitch.

YOU WILL NEED

- 6 glass bottles—all the same size
- A small metal rod or stick
- Water
- Masking tape
- A pen
- A ruler

STEPS

1 CLEAN THE BOTTLES OUT THOROUGHLY, then empty them so there's no water inside. Label each bottle with numbers from 1 to 6.

2 FILL EACH BOTTLE WITH THE FOLLOWING LEVELS OF WATER, using your ruler to measure: Bottle 1 should have 5 ½ inches (14 cm) of water. Bottle 2 should have 4 inches (10 cm). Bottle 3 should have 3 ½ inches (8.5 cm). Bottle 4 should have 3 inches (7.5 cm). Fill bottle 5 to 2 ½ inches (6.5 cm). And fill bottle 6 just 2 inches (5 cm).

3 TAP EACH BOTTLE LIGHTLY WITH A METAL ROD or stick and notice the different pitches they produce—it's like having your own xylophone. If you fill each bottle correctly, you can tap them in a particular order to play a tune. You can either make up your own songs, or play some old favorites.

Playing a tune

Here's how to play a couple of simple old songs to try out your bottle orchestra. First of all, here's the order of bottle taps you need to play *Mary Had A Little Lamb*:

> 3212333
> 222
> 355
> 3212333
> 122321

And this is how you'd play *Row, Row, Row Your Boat*:

> 11123
> 32345
> 66553311
> 54321

Blowing on the bottles

Another way to make music with bottles is to blow across their tops. Some people use large jugs to get a deep baritone sound from a bottle. These people sometimes form bands known as "jug bands."

If you blow across the top of your water-filled bottles you'll get different notes, just like you would if you tapped on them with a stick. The difference is the pitch of the notes will be the exact opposite of when you tapped on them. The bottle with the most water is going to give a high note while the bottle with the least amount of water is going to give a low note. Why? Because by blowing on a bottle you're making the air inside it vibrate, not the glass bottle itself. A small amount of air (just like a small amount of water) is going to have a high pitch and a large amount of air (just like a large amount of water) is going to have a low pitch. The more a bottle is filled with water, the less air it has inside it and the higher the pitch.

Panpipes

❧ ❧

A more traditional musical instrument, based on the same principle as bottle music, is the panpipes. They have been in use for thousands of years in civilizations all across the world.

In ancient Greece they were made out of reeds and associated with the woodland god Pan (which is where they get their modern name). In the Andes, they are made from bamboo and known as *siku* or *zampoña*.

YOU WILL NEED
- A piece of plastic pipe 49 inches (123 cm) long and ½ inch (1.2 cm) in diameter
- A small saw
- Modeling clay
- A tape measure
- Sticky tape

STEPS

1 YOU'RE GOING TO CUT YOUR PLASTIC PIPING into five panpipes, so measure out the following lengths: 12 ½ inches (31 cm), 11 inches (28 cm), 10 inches (25 cm), 8 ½ inches (21 cm), and 7 inches (18 cm). Use the saw to cut the lengths out as smoothly as possible.

2 SEAL THE BOTTOM OF EACH PIPE with modeling clay. Make sure no air can get out through the bottom.

3 UNROLL A PIECE OF TAPE 5 inches (12.5 cm) long and lay it, sticky-side up, on the table. Arrange the pipes in order of size in the middle of the tape, making sure to keep the top ends (the ends without the clay) at the same level.

4 WRAP THE REST OF THE TAPE round the front of your set of pipes and you're ready to play. Blow gently across the top of a pipe. Don't blow too hard, and don't blow down into the pipe. If you can't get a sound out, make sure the bottom of the pipe is sealed. Try to work out some tunes.

A kaleidoscope

⚜ ⚜

"Kaleidoscope" comes from the Greek words that mean "beautiful view," and that's just what you get when you look through the end of one of these tubes. But the view isn't of a magical and colorful island in the clouds. You're looking at a collection of shiny bits of paper and beads that are reflected many times by a set of mirrors.

All you need to make your own kaleidoscope (and the beautiful view that comes with it) is a few simple materials, and about an hour.

YOU WILL NEED
- Cardboard
- Scissors
- 3 small rectangular mirrors
- Clear tape
- Tracing paper
- Very small, shiney, and colorful bits of paper cut into fun shapes
- A pencil

STEPS

1 PLACE EACH MIRROR ON A SHEET OF CARDBOARD and trace around it with a pencil, drawing as close to the edge of the mirror as you can.

2 CUT THE CARDBOARD ALONG THE PENCIL lines so that you end up with three rectangular pieces of cardboard the same size as your mirrors.

3 TAPE THE MIRRORS TO THE CARDBOARD CUTOUTS. Try not to get too much tape on the front of the mirrors or you'll see it in your view.

4 CREATE A TRIANGULAR TUBE by taping all three pieces of cardboard and mirror together. The mirrors should be facing inward, and you should tape them as tightly together as you can so there are no gaps.

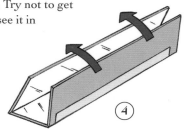

5 CUT OUT TWO TRIANGULAR PIECES of tracing paper that will fit exactly over the end of the triangular tube. Tape these pieces of tracing paper together on two sides so that you form a triangular envelope.

6 FILL THE TRIANGULAR ENVELOPE with small bits of shiny paper cutouts through the un-taped side. Don't overfill it—you want to allow the shiny bits of paper to move around freely inside.

7 WHEN THE ENVELOPE IS FILLED to your liking, tape the third side of it closed to seal in the shiny bits of paper. Then tape the triangle over one end of the kaleidoscope tube.

8 NEXT, CUT OUT A TRIANGULAR PIECE of cardboard to fit over the opposite end of the tube and tape it in place.

9 USE YOUR PENCIL and poke an eyehole into the triangular cardboard end. Your kaleidoscope is now ready.

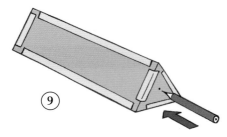

10 TO USE THE KALEIDOSCOPE, point it toward the light and look through the eyehole. The light coming into the tube will reflect off the mirrors and create symmetrical patterns around the little bits of paper. To get a new design, shake the kaleidoscope and look again.

DID YOU KNOW? The kaleidoscope was originally conceived by ancient Greek mathematicians. But the knowledge was lost over the centuries, until it was reinvented in 1816 by a Scottish scientist called David Brewster. He originally designed it as a science experiment, but it quickly became more popular and famous as a toy.

Table football

❧

If you're an explorer looking for a little competition, look no further. Here's a game that will let you recreate the glory of Super Bowls past. Kick field goals, score touchdowns, and do it all without even lacing up your sneakers. Welcome to the great world of table football, where the right paper fold and a sure hand will lead you to victory over your friends and anyone else who thinks their game is better than yours.

The construction part comes in making the football, which shouldn't take you too long. The rest of the game . . . well, let's say you might need a little rest from constructing, every now and again.

YOU WILL NEED

- A sheet of paper
- A pair of scissors
- A table
- A friend to play with

Make the football

1 TAKE AN 8½ X 11-INCH (21- X 28-CM) sheet of medium-weight printer paper and cut it in half lengthways.

2 TAKE ONE HALF, AND FOLD IT IN HALF LENGTHWAYS, to give you a long thin strip of paper.

3 STARTING AT ONE END, make a triangle by folding the corner back onto itself and lining up the folded end with the top of the strip.

4 NOW MAKE THE TRIANGLE THICK and strong by folding it up and over on itself all the way up the length of the paper.

5 WHEN YOU REACH THE END OF THE PAPER, tuck the flap of extra paper into the pocket on the other side of the triangle football. Now you're ready to play.

Rules of the game

1 TABLE FOOTBALL IS PLAYED BETWEEN TWO PLAYERS who sit across a table from each other. You score points by kicking field goals (three points), scoring touchdowns (six points), and kicking extra points after touchdowns (one point). The first person to score 35 points wins.

2 DETERMINE WHO GOES FIRST BY FLIPPING A COIN. The winner receives the kick off.

3 TO KICK OFF, HOLD THE PAPER FOOTBALL in the palm of your hand and gently toss it onto the table toward the opposing player's end. You must release the football from your end of the table—do not reach across the table over the opposing player's side of the "field."

4 PLAY STARTS WHEREVER THE FOOTBALL LANDS. If it falls off the end of the table, the player who is receiving the football may place it on the table two hand lengths from his end.

5 ADVANCE THE FOOTBALL toward the opposing player's side of the table by either flicking it with an index finger or hitting it with your index and middle fingers held together. Excess "pushing" of the football is not allowed. Each player gets one flick and then it's the opposing player's turn. The aim is to score points by making a touchdown.

6 TO SCORE A TOUCHDOWN you must hit the football with just enough force that it overhangs the opposing player's side of the table without falling off. If any portion of the football hangs over the edge of the table, it's a touchdown and you get six points. You are then allowed an attempt to kick a field goal for an extra point.

7 TO KICK AN EXTRA POINT the opposing player makes goal posts by putting his wrists on the table, placing his thumbs end to end and raising his index fingers into the air.

8 YOU MUST "KICK" THE FOOTBALL from the middle of the table. Do this by holding the football on the table, point down and flicking the football towards the upright index fingers. If it passes anywhere between your opponent's "goal" fingers in the air, then you've scored.

9 IT'S ALSO POSSIBLE FOR A PLAYER TO SCORE three points by kicking a field goal. A field goal attempt, however, can only come if the opposing player hits the football out of bounds three times. If the football goes off the sides or ends of the table, that's considered out of bounds. After the third out of bounds the count starts over. Kick a field goal in the same way you kick an extra point.

10 IF YOU SCORE A TOUCHDOWN OR FIELD GOAL, you kick off to the opposing player just as though the game is starting. You must also kick off if you hit the football out of bounds (as long you have not yet done that three times.)

11 IT'S ALSO POSSIBLE TO PLAY PAPER FOOTBALL against the clock. Set a timer to 10 minutes and whoever has the most points at the end of that time wins. If the score is tied, determine the winner by kicking 10 field goals, trading turns after each kick. Whoever has the most field goals at the end of 10 turns wins.

DID YOU KNOW? If you've beaten all your friends and want to try your paper-football skills out with a different crowd, consider joining the United States Paper Football Association and competing in one of their annual nationwide tournaments.

If you really enjoy paper football, you might be interested to know that rules have been developed for paper soccer, paper basketball, paper baseball, and even paper golf! It's amazing how many field games can be adapted for playing on a tabletop with some folded paper. Why not make up your own rules and set up competitions? See if you can invent a sport as popular as paper football.

A jigsaw puzzle

⚜

If you're the kind of person who really likes to fix things, then jigsaw puzzles are for you. But what if you like to break stuff? Making your own jigsaw puzzle is a good mix between the two. You get to cut up a photograph or work of art into a bunch of tiny pieces. Then if you want to, you can put it back together. Or, if you prefer, hand it over to a friend and leave it to them to puzzle it out.

The cool thing about using photographs for your jigsaw puzzle is you can take lots of different ones with a digital camera—of people, objects, animals, whatever— and then print them out on your computer. Just be sure to use photo or card stock rather than regular printer paper, which is too thin for your puzzle pieces. And always make sure you've got another copy somewhere of the picture you cut up, just in case your jigsaw goes wrong.

YOU WILL NEED ⚠

- 8½ x 11-inch (21- x 28-cm) piece of thick posterboard
- A photograph or painting printed to about the same size
- Glue or mounting spray
- Sheets of newspaper
- A pencil
- A utility knife with a fresh, sharp blade

STEPS

1 ATTACH THE PHOTOGRAPH to the piece of posterboard using glue. The best stuff to use is mounting spray. This can be bought at a craft store and is better than regular glue because it gives you an overall seal— a good thing when you start to cut the photo up into small pieces.

WARNING

Always follow instructions carefully when using mounting spray. Only use it in well-ventilated spaces and never directly inhale it.

Always put a sheet or two of newspaper down before using the spray, because it can cause a mess.

2 COVER THE POSTERBOARD with another sheet of newspaper, and place a thick book on top of the photograph to make sure it sticks to the cardboard evenly and securely and that there are no air bubbles in the glue.

3 WHEN THE GLUE HAS DRIED, turn the posterboard over so the photo is face-down. On the back, draw out the pieces of your puzzle with a pencil. Avoid giving your pieces very small ends or sharp points, because these can get damaged too easily. However, try to make each piece different so that they'll only fit together one way.

4 WITH THE POSTERBOARD FACE STILL FACE DOWN, make sure you have a working surface under it that can be cut with a utility knife. Your mother's dining room table is not a good place for this, unless you use a sheet of plywood on top of it to protect it.

5 WITH YOUR UTILITY KNIFE at a 90-degree angle to the poster board, cut along the lines to make the individual puzzle pieces.

6 WHEN YOU'RE DONE make sure all the pieces fit—if you can figure out how they match up!

DID YOU KNOW? Jigsaw puzzles were originally created in the 1760s by mapmakers who used them to teach their students about geography. The name comes—unsurprisingly—from a tool called a jigsaw, which has a thin blade that can be used to cut out complicated shapes like jigsaw pieces.

Jigsaws are no longer sawn out of wood piece by piece. These days, special machines are made with blades in the shape of the jigsaw pieces. The picture is printed onto a card or wooden backing and then placed under the press, which forces the blades through the puzzle at very high pressures. The more pieces there are in the puzzle, the greater the length of blade that must be forced through the board.

Paper hats

❧❧

People have been wearing hats for thousands of years and the reasons for wearing them are as varied as the styles of the hats. Hats can keep the sun and rain off. They can keep a head warm. They can hide hair or bald heads. And of course they can provide some plain old fun.

Discover the folded ins and outs of paper hat-making and you can turn a boring get together into a goofy good time. A single sheet of newspaper is all you need to create several different kinds of headgear. With these simple instructions you can make a pirate's hat, a bishop's hat, or a military hat, and you can do it in 15 or 20 minutes.

You can just goof around with these, or you can put together a play with different hats for different characters. If you really like the designs, why not paint them in the right colors for the job to help with building up your characters? Black with a skull and crossbones is good for pirates, red or purple for bishops, and green or khaki for the military hat.

YOU WILL NEED
● Several sheets of newspaper

Pirate hat

1 TAKE A SINGLE NEWSPAPER SHEET and fold it in half (this is the way it comes in the newspaper anyway.)

2 FOLD IT IN HALF AGAIN HORIZONTALLY, leaving the new crease at the top—the bottom should be left open.

3 FOLD BOTH THE TOP CORNERS IN toward the middle of the paper so that they meet. You should now have a triangle with a pointed top and a flap on the bottom.

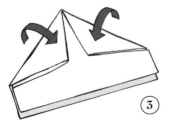

4 FOLD THE TOP SIDE of the bottom flap up.

5 FLIP THE HAT OVER and wrap the corner of the flap you've just folded around to the back of the hat.

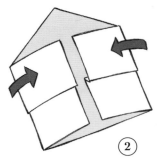

6 NOW FOLD THE REMAINING FLAP UP, flip the hat over and wrap the corners of that flap around to the other side of the hat. You should now have a triangle that opens at the bottom.

7 OPEN THE HAT UP, put it on, and—Arrrggghhh!—you're a pirate!

Bishop's hat

1 FOLLOW THE INSTRUCTIONS for the pirate hat through to step 4.

2 THEN FLIP THE HAT OVER and fold the sides of the hat in toward the middle so that you're left with a piece of paper that looks like a house. How far in you fold the sides will depend on how big your head is—each side will probably only fold in about 2 inches (5 cm).

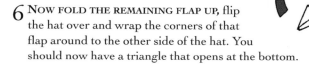
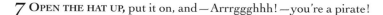

3 NOW FOLD THE BOTTOM TWO CORNERS in so that you're left with a point at the bottom of the house-shaped paper.

4 FOLD THE TIP OF THE BOTTOM POINT UP and tuck it behind the side folds so it's held in place (otherwise your hat will fall apart when you put it on.)

5 OPEN THE HAT UP, PUT IT ON, and you're a bishop.

Military hat

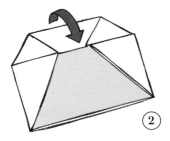

1 FOLLOW THE BISHOP'S HAT INSTRUCTIONS all the way through to step 4.

2 ONLY NOW, FOLD THE ROOF POINT of the house-shaped paper down so that the end of the tip tucks into the side folds on top of the bottom point, and you're done.

3 PUT IT ON AND MARCH AROUND like a proper soldier.

Hats like these are great for quick and easy costumes, because their shapes are associated with particular job titles or ranks. This is nothing new — historical evidence shows hats being used to show a person's importance as far back as Ancient Egypt and China.

You can use these hats as the basis for a short play or sketch, or for games. One game involves four people and one of each type of hat. Three of the people get one hat each, and have to act the role of the person who owns that hat — a pirate, a bishop, or a soldier. They should most preferably put on silly voices for each character, and make sure to use the right sort of language: for example, lots of "ship-shape" and "shiver-me-timbers" for the pirate, and lots of "sir-yes-sir" for the soldier.

The fourth person comes up with a scenario in which those three people might find themselves together, and the other three people have to act it out while staying in character. The fourth person periodically switches the hats around, and each actor has to change his character to match whatever hat he's wearing. If he gets it wrong, he swaps places with the fourth person, and takes his turn to make up a scenario and switch the hats around.

DID YOU KNOW? A "hatter" is the name given to makers of men's hats (if you make women's hats you are a "milliner"). The Mad Hatter in *Alice's Adventures in Wonderland* gets his name from the fact that hat makers in the eighteenth and nineteenth centuries used to work with a chemical solution called nitrate of mercury, which would damage the brain if used indoors without any ventilation, and result in mental illness. The expression "mad as a hatter" comes from the same source.

Papier mâché

❧❧❧

The Chinese were the first to invent paper, so it makes sense that they were the first to invent papier mâché. The modern name comes from French and means "chewed paper." Supposedly, French workers in English paper shops would chew on paper to moisten it so they could make papier mâché constructions.

Papier mâché has been such around a long time, and it's such a great material for constructing things, because it's easy to work with, is lightweight, and can be painted. All you need to tackle a project is an idea, some newspaper, and some flour and water for the paste. Once you have these, whatever shape you can dream up can be created.

The paste

This is the basis of your papier mâché. You'll need to make plenty of it for any project you start.

YOU WILL NEED
- A large mixing bowl
- All-purpose flour
- Salt
- Water

Steps

1 MIX ONE PART FLOUR TO ABOUT TWO PARTS WATER in a large mixing bowl. You're going for the consistency of gravy—not too thick and not too watery. If it's too thick it's difficult to work with. If it's too watery it'll take your project forever to dry.

2 STIR THE MIXTURE until you get all the lumps out.

3 ADD IN A TABLESPOON OF SALT for each part flour. This helps prevent mold from growing on your models.

Papier mâché mask

This is a project anyone can do, though it takes some detailed work and about two days to complete, mostly because you have to let the papier mâché dry. Papier mâché masks can be painted in any design you like, so they're great for spooky Halloween costumes.

YOU WILL NEED

- A round balloon
- Newspaper strips roughly 2 inches (5 cm) wide
- Papier mâché paste
- An old bowl
- Tin foil
- Masking tape
- Paint

STEPS

1 THIS IS MESSY WORK so cover your work area with a plastic table cloth or sheets of newspaper.

2 BLOW UP THE BALLOON TO THE DESIRED SIZE — you want it to be a bit larger than your head, so that you'll be able to fit the mask comfortably over your face when it's done.

3 EXCEPT FOR A HEAD-SIZED HOLE IN THE BOTTOM, cover the balloon with a layer of newspaper strips dipped in the paste. Hold one end of a newspaper strip and run it lengthways through the paste. As it comes out, use the thumb and forefinger of your other hand to squeeze off the excess paste.

4 COVER THE WHOLE THING IN THREE LAYERS of newspaper strips — any more than that and it'll take forever to dry. Then place the covered balloon in an old bowl, propped so that it stays upright, and leave it overnight to dry completely.

5 WHEN THE "HEAD" HAS DRIED, repeat step 4 again with another three layers of papier mâché, and leave it to dry again.

6 WHEN IT HAS COMPLETELY DRIED, pop the balloon. Now you should have a sturdy base for your mask. Put it over your head and carefully mark the positions of your eyes, nose and mouth on the outside with a pencil. Take the mask off and poke the pencil through to make eye-, nose-, and mouth-holes.

7 NOW USE MORE PAPIER MÂCHÉ to model monstrous features around the eyes, nose and mouth. Use your imagination to create something really scary! When it's dry, paint over the top to make a realistic monster face.

8 THE MASK should now be ready to wear.

Papier mâché box

Ever wanted to make your own pirate treasure chest or magic box? Here's how. This project is a little easier than the mask. You still have to let it dry though, so it might take a while to complete.

YOU WILL NEED

- Strips of newspaper
- Papier mâché paste
- Cardboard
- Masking tape
- Scissors or utility knife

STEPS

1 CUT OUT PIECES OF CARDBOARD to make a box or rectangle with four sides and a bottom (we'll make the lid later). Use masking tape to tape it all together.

2 COVER THE CARDBOARD IN PAPIER MÂCHÉ using the same technique as for the mask. Start by covering the top lip of the box with a single strip of newspaper so that it's smooth. Cover the inside as well as the outside, then set the box aside to dry.

3 WHILE IT'S DRYING, cut out a piece of cardboard for the lid. It should be slightly larger than the box top opening. Also, cut out ½-inch- (1-cm-) wide strips of cardboard to fit around the lid as lips. Tape the lips to the lid and cover it all in papier mâché.

4 ADD AT LEAST TWO MORE LAYERS of papier mâché to the box and lid, and mold it into iron bands and a hefty padlock for a treasure chest, or mystical swirls and symbols for a magic box. Leave it to dry thoroughly, then paint it to fit the patterns you've molded on it.

A whirligig

In the old days, the British used a whirligig as a form of punishment for disobedient soldiers. Back then it was a box suspended by a rope. The condemned soldier would be put into the box and spun around as quickly as possible until he got sick.

These days, however, a whirligig is just a toy for making colored patterns. Making a toy whirligig is easy—so easy that you can make one for all your friends. Or they're a nice present for a younger brother, to stop him pestering you. You can do each one in about 30 minutes.

YOU WILL NEED

- A stiff piece of cardboard
- A pair of scissors
- A pencil
- Paints or coloring pens or pencils
- About 2 feet (60 cm) of string

STEPS

1 DRAW A 6-INCH- (15-CM-) DIAMETER CIRCLE on a piece of cardboard and cut it out. Decorate the cut-out however you like. You can draw a single line spiraling out from the center, paint on a giant triangle or square, or simply put on lots of different colors.

2 PUNCH TWO SMALL HOLES opposite each other about ¼ inch (0.5 cm) from the center of the circle. Run a piece of string through both holes and tie the ends together to make a loop.

3 HOLD EACH END OF THE STRINGS between the thumb and index fingers of both hands and position the cardboard cut-out in the middle.

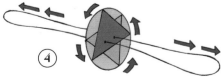

4 TO MAKE IT SPIN, relax the string a little then pull it taut. Continue doing this until you get a good fast spin.

Puppets

✦✦

Hundreds of years ago, puppets and their handlers—known as puppeteers—would travel the countryside putting on puppet shows for a few coins for whoever would sit and watch. Kids loved it, but most people considered puppet shows to be a crude and unskilled form of entertainment.

The fact is, puppeteers have a very difficult job. They have to act with their hands. They also have to know how to operate lots of different kinds of puppets. There are marionettes, which are puppets controlled from above by many different strings; and there are shadow puppets on sticks, hand puppets of all different kinds, ventriloquist's dummies, finger puppets, and many more.

Making some of the more complicated puppets is a job better left to professional puppeteers, but here are two that you can make yourself. All you need are a few household items and a couple hours of constructing time.

Shadow puppets

Shadow puppets were invented in the Far East hundreds of years ago, and are still very popular in countries like India and Indonesia. They are wood, leather, or cardboard cutouts that make shadows on a wall or a white screen.

YOU WILL NEED

- Cardboard
- A pencil
- Scissors
- Glue
- Popsicle sticks
- A sheet or white wall
- A lamp

STEPS

1 DRAW THE OUTLINE OF YOUR FAVORITE ANIMAL on a piece of cardboard. If you aren't a good artist, find a picture on the Internet, print it out, then glue it to the cardboard. Make the puppet at least as large as your open hand, if not larger.

2 CUT OUT THE PUPPET following the outline of the animal figure.

3 GLUE A POPSICLE STICK onto the middle of one side of the puppet. This will be your handle.

4 FOR A MORE COMPLICATED PUPPET, make the arms separately and fix them to the puppet's shoulders with paper fasteners. Attach popsicle sticks to the hands so you can move the arms independent of the body.

5 THERE ARE TWO WAYS TO PUT ON A DISPLAY with your shadow puppets: One is to shine a lamp onto a white wall and use your puppets to make shadows on it.

6 THE OTHER IS TO FIX UP A SHEET across a doorway and sit behind it with your puppets and the lamp. Make sure your audience is on the other side. Shine the lamp on the sheet, and use the popsicle sticks to hold the puppets against the lit area—they'll make a silhouette on the other side for your audience to see.

7 MAKE MULTIPLE CHARACTERS and get a few friends together to operate them and provide voices. Then you can stage a full play.

Sock puppet

For something a little less serious, and a bit easier, one of the funnest puppets to make is a sock puppet. Here's how to put one together in about a half hour.

YOU WILL NEED
- An old sock
- Some colorful felt or cardboard
- Scissors
- Glue or needle and thread

STEPS

1 PLACE A SOCK OVER YOUR HAND and tuck part of the toe-end in between your thumb and outstretched fingers. This creates a mouth. (Make sure it's a clean sock!)

2 CUT OUT A RED OR PINK TRIANGULAR PIECE OF CLOTH for a nose, and two round black bits of cloth for eyes.

3 USING THE MOUTH AS A REFERENCE, glue or sew the pieces of cloth onto you sock puppet in the right places to make a face.

4 TO MAKE A SNAKE, cut out a long red tongue and glue or sew it in place inside the mouth. For a dog, bear, or other animal, use a round pink piece as a tongue.

5 MAKE TRIANGULAR EARS and attach them to the top.

6 FOR A MORE PERMANENT SOCK PUPPET, cut out two pieces of cardboard for the top and bottom parts of the mouth and glue them in place.

7 TO MAKE THE PUPPET "TALK" simply move your fingers and thumb up and down as if the puppet's mouth were moving.

8 MAKE UP SOME FUNNY PHRASES and a silly voice for your puppet and try cracking some jokes. You'll be a stage ventriloquist in no time!

Make a puppet stage

To give yourself a performance space, tack up a sheet across a doorway so that it covers your head when you stand up. The puppets can perform over the top.

YOU WILL NEED

- A doorway
- A sheet
- Thumbtacks

STEPS

1 KNEEL ON THE FLOOR IN THE DOORWAY in a comfortable position for performing with your puppets. Work out how high the sheet will have to be so that your audience can't see you as you perform.

2 USE THUMBTACKS TO ATTACH THE SHEET on either side of the doorframe so it covers you kneeling behind it. Use the top of the sheet as "floor level" for your puppets during the show.

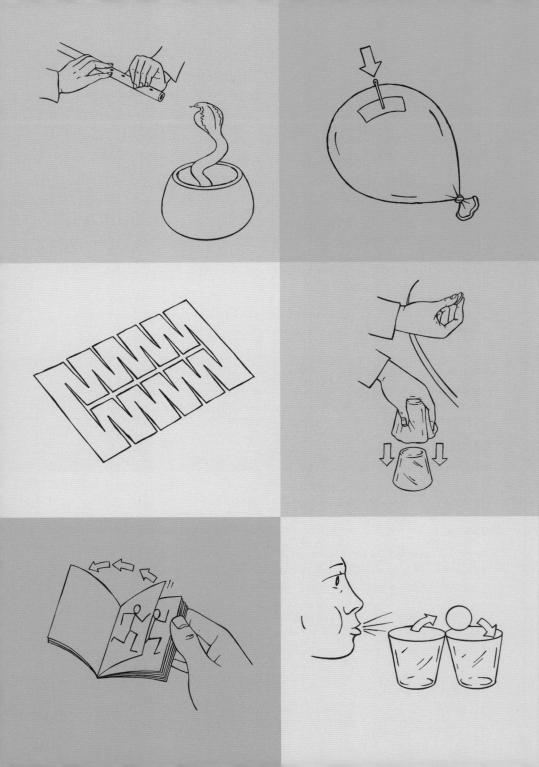

Chapter Four

Tricking

A MAGICIAN ONCE SAID TO HIS APPRENTICE,
"discovery for you is discovery for your audience."
Exploring and discovering new things doesn't
have to be a solitary science. Take some time to
show off what you learn. Science experiments can
often seem magical. You can easily duplicate a few
on stage in the name of magic, and explore new
ways to wow your friends

✦

Sometimes an explorer needs a few tricks up his
sleeve, to make friends or distract potential
enemies. But don't forget, while illusions and
sleight of hand are the tools of all illusionists,
magicians, and escape artists, none of them would
be worth the rabbits in their hats if they didn't
have a special flair for putting on a good show.

Stink bombs

✦

What better way to make a quick escape than to stun the enemy with a stink bomb? This foul-smelling trick is really not a bomb at all—at least in the sense that you won't be lighting a fuse and watching an explosion. It's more of a theoretical "bomb." But what an impact it has. Just mix together a few chemicals, put them in a cup and leave the lid off. Your foes will be running for the hills (and the fresh air) in no time.

This is an easy project that takes less than 10 minutes, once you have the right ingredients, all of which can be found at a grocery or health food store.

YOU WILL NEED
- Distilled white vinegar
- Cup or bottle with a lid
- Valerian root capsules

STEPS

1 TAKE THIS OUTSIDE, because the smell can permeate indoor furnishings and ruin them, which won't make your parents happy! Empty three capsules of valerian root into the cup or bottle. Valerian is a herb used to combat stress —it also smells pretty bad.

2 ADD A TABLESPOON OR TWO (15–30 ML) OF VINEGAR. This is where the lid becomes important—put it tightly on your container and swirl the vinegar and valerian powder so they mix thoroughly.

3 KEEP THE CONTAINER SEALED until you're ready to use it. Pour the mixture out on the ground upwind of your target and wait for the smell to blow over to them.

Balloon tricks

❖ ❖

There's something about balloons that inspires all kinds of tricks. Maybe it's because they come in so many different shapes and colors, or because clowns can twist them into dogs, swords, hats, and other funny configurations. Maybe it's because we like the unexpected pop when a balloon meets its end. Whatever the cause, balloon tricks are some of the best crowd-pleasers in the book. So grab some balloons and try these out next time you need to make a friend during your explorations (or make a splash at your little brother's birthday party).

Pop-proof balloon

One sure-fire way to pop a balloon is to stick a needle in it. Works every time. A good trick, then, is to stick a needle in a balloon without popping it. Think it can't be done? Read on.

YOU WILL NEED

- 2 dark-colored balloons
- Clear sticky tape

- A needle or two

STEPS

1 BEFORE YOUR SHOW, blow up two dark-colored balloons to a good size and tie them off.

2 THEN TAKE ONE OF THE BALLOONS and stick one or more strips of tape onto one side or the top.

3 START YOUR TRICK BY SAYING SOMETHING LIKE "everyone knows a needle will pop a balloon, right?" and then use a needle to demonstrate how this works. Stick a needle in the normal balloon so that it pops.

4 THEN ANNOUNCE that you will now use your magical powers to protect the next balloon from the sharp point of the needle.

5 SAY A FEW MAGIC WORDS and stick your needle into the balloon through the center of one strip of tape. It won't pop! For a more dramatic effect, let go of the needle so that it's sticking out of the balloon.

6 IF YOU PUT MORE THAN ONE STRIP of tape on the balloon, leave the first needle in the balloon and stick a second needle into the balloon through a different strip of tape.

7 AFTER THIS, let the audience know you will now remove your magic protection of the balloon—take out the two "magic" needles, and stick one into the balloon somewhere there isn't any tape, to pop it. This also destroys any evidence of the tape, so nobody can tell how the trick was done.

Fireproof balloon

If a needle can pop a balloon then fire certainly can, can't it? Not always. Try this easy trick to wow your audience.

YOU WILL NEED

- A balloon
- ½ a cup (120 ml) of water

- A funnel
- A match

STEPS

1 USE A FUNNEL TO POUR THE WATER into an un-inflated balloon.

2 CAREFULLY BLOW UP the balloon and tie it off.

3 LIGHT A MATCH and hold it under the part of the balloon where the

WARNING

As always, you should be extremely careful and have adult supervision when using matches or playing with fire.

water is settled. It won't pop, because the water absorbs the heat through the rubber wall of the balloon. In fact, you can even touch the lit match to the part of the balloon where the water has settled and it still won't pop.

Self-inflating balloon

Sometimes one of the funniest parts of any balloon trick is watching how red in the face the magician or clown gets blowing up 20 balloons in a row. Using those stomach muscles to empty your lungs time after time can get tiring. So why not do a trick that can blow a balloon up for you? This project takes about 5 minutes to set up, and about 1 minute for the balloon to fully inflate.

YOU WILL NEED

- A large round balloon
- An empty large plastic soda bottle
- 2 cups (450 ml) distilled white vinegar
- A funnel
- A sheet of paper
- Baking soda

STEPS

1 POUR A FINGER-WIDTH LINE of baking soda down the middle of the paper.

2 THEN ROLL THE PAPER INTO A TIGHT TUBE and fold the ends so the baking soda won't fall out.

3 DROP THE PAPER TUBE into the soda bottle.

4 PLACE A FUNNEL INTO THE OPENING of the soda bottle and pour in the vinegar.

5 QUICKLY REMOVE THE FUNNEL and stretch the mouth of your balloon over the mouth of the soda bottle.

6 NEXT, PICK UP THE BOTTLE and shake it rapidly for 20 seconds. The vinegar will mix with the baking soda to produce carbon dioxide gas. As the gas pressure inside the bottle increases, the balloon will inflate — *voila*!

The jumping ping-pong ball

Sometimes you can turn the simplest science into a nifty little trick. Here's one that uses Bernoulli's principle, the same notion scientists use to describe how airplanes fly (see page 52). When air flows over a wing it creates a lower pressure than the air under it, causing lift. When you blow over a glass, a ping-pong ball will lift out of it because of the same principle. With a few tries you may even be able to lift the ping-pong ball into another glass. And you thought all magicians were just full of hot air!

YOU WILL NEED
- Two glasses
- A ping-pong ball

STEPS

1 PLACE TWO GLASSES right next to each other, one in front of the other, so that they touch.

2 PUT A PING-PONG BALL in the front glass.

3 BLOW AT AN ANGLE ACROSS THE TOP of the glass and watch as the ball hops out of the glass and into the next one.

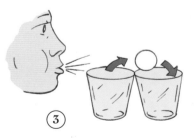

The fast air moving over the top of the glasses creates an area of low pressure just above the ping-pong ball. This pulls the ball up into the stream of air, which pushes it along into the second glass. If you blow hard enough, it'll get sucked out of this glass as well and roll away.

Putting your head through a postcard

✦ ✦

If you're staging a magic show, hold up a postcard and say "who thinks I'm going to be able to fit my head through this piece of card?" You'll likely get silence, which is what you want—afterall, part of a good magic trick is doing something no one believes you can do. If you're performing this trick in front of a group of people be sure and come up with a few jokes or a story to tell while you're making the cuts. It can take about 15 minutes to get all the cuts right, and you don't want them to get bored. While you cut, you could tell a story about a mythical tailor who used this technique to make magical clothes using only postcard-sized pieces of cloth, or a magician who escaped from prison by turning a mouse-hole into an escape tunnel using the method you're about to demonstrate.

You might want to practice this trick in private a couple times first, too, before trying it out in front of an audience, because the whole thing unravels if you get any of the cuts wrong.

YOU WILL NEED
- A postcard or a piece of paper about 3 x 5 inches (7 x 12 cm)
- A pair of scissors
- Good cutting skills

STEPS

1 CARD WORKS BETTER THAN PAPER for this trick because it's more durable and less likely to fall apart while you're cutting. Start off by folding the postcard in half lengthways.

2 USE A PAIR OF SCISSORS and make six evenly-spaced cuts about 1 inch (2.5 cm) deep at regular intervals along the ridge of the fold. Cut down from the fold toward the edge, but be sure not to cut all the way through or your card will fall to pieces and you'll have to start over.

3 THEN MAKE SIX 1-inch (2.5-cm) cuts along the edge of the postcard opposite the fold. Be sure and make these cuts in the middle of the cuts you made in step two.

4 OPEN THE FOLD UP to reveal six deep cuts in the middle of the postcard and six cuts on both edges.

5 NOW CAREFULLY CUT THE POSTCARD along where the fold used to be, but be sure to cut only from the edge of the first cut closest to the middle. Do not cut all the way through or you'll have to start over!

6 AFTER THIS YOU CAN GENTLY OPEN UP the card into a large paper loop that will fit around your head, and maybe even your whole body.

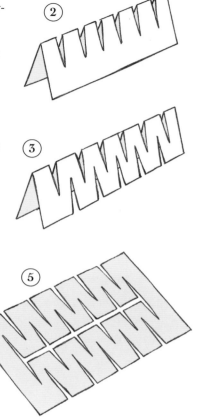

7 IF YOUR CARD WON'T OPEN UP, try folding it back in half and making the cuts from steps 2 and 3 a bit deeper.

Of course, you haven't really made the postcard any bigger — you can prove this by weighing the card before and after the trick, to show that it always has exactly the same amount of material in it. All you've done is to give the surface area of the card (the size of its flat edge) the longest perimeter (the distance around the outside edges) as possible.

The levitating teabag

Sometimes pulling off a good trick has a lot to do with how you present it. By saying you plan to "levitate" a teabag, you conjure up images of floating wizards and hovering young assistants. But really all you're doing is striking a match and lighting an empty teabag on fire. That's why "levitating" has such a nice ring. No one wants to watch you just light a teabag on fire.

YOU WILL NEED

- An unused teabag
- Scissors
- Matches

- An old plate
- An empty container (or teapot)

STEPS

1 CAREFULLY CUT THE TOP OFF of the teabag with some scissors.

2 GENTLY UNFOLD THE BAG and pour the tealeaves out into an empty container. Then cut off the bottom and open the teabag out.

3 IN ITS UNFOLDED STATE, the teabag is really just a long cylinder. Stand the cylinder on its end in the middle of a plate.

4 STRIKE A MATCH and light the top of the teabag cylinder on fire.

5 AS IT BURNS DOWN, the teabag gets lighter, while the air around it heats up. Since hot air rises, the burnt and lightweight teabag gets carried up with the hot air and momentarily levitates above the table.

W A R N I N G

Never use matches without proper supervision. Always make sure nothing nearby can catch fire.

The levitating olive

✦✦✦

In this trick the olive really does levitate momentarily before you catch it in a glass. There is no sleight of hand or magic taking place, though. It's all science. Specifically it's the science of centrifugal force, which is the force that acts on an object following a circular path at a constant speed. Watch and you'll be amazed—and so will your audience.

This trick takes some practice and patience, so don't get frustrated on the first, second, or even third try. And as always, when you're ready to perform, say a little "hocus pocus" at the right moment as you do it, to impress your audience.

YOU WILL NEED
- An olive
- A round wine glass
- A smooth table

STEPS

1 START BY TELLING YOUR AUDIENCE you will put the olive in the glass without touching it. Place an olive on the table and put the the glass upside-down on the table over the olive.

2 WITH THE GLASS TOUCHING THE TABLE TOP, rotate it in circles around the olive, so that the olive rolls around the sides of the glass.

3 WHEN YOU DO THIS YOU CREATE CENTRIFUGAL FORCE inside the glass as the walls push the olive inwards. If you gradually increase the speed, the olive should at first roll around the walls of the glass, then slowly start moving up the walls and into the center of the glass.

4 WHEN THE OLIVE IS SPINNING AROUND right under the center of the glass, quickly turn the glass over. If you get it right, the olive will "stick" in the bottom of the glass as you turn it over. Shazam!

Pushing a glass through a table

✦✦

Now we're getting into the *real* tricks. There's no science going on here. Just some good old sleight of hand—one of the most important skills a magician can master. Now's also the time to pump up your showmanship. The key to this trick is to distract your audience from what's really going on.

As always, the best way to do this is to talk. You might think magicians' "patter"—the jokes and stories they tell the audience—is just for entertainment, but it's more than that. They use it to direct the audience's attention to where they want it—i.e. away from where the trick is *really* going on.

YOU WILL NEED

- A glass
- A thick paper napkin large enough to cover the glass completely
- A table
- A chair to sit on
- A coin

STEPS

1 YOU HAVE TO BE SEATED TO DO THIS TRICK—you'll find out why in a moment.

2 ONCE YOU'RE COMFORTABLY SEATED at the table, announce to your audience that you will now magically make a solid pass through a solid.

3 THEN PLACE THE COIN on the table and place the glass over the coin. Announce that it's impossible for you to reach the coin.

WARNING

Make sure your audience are all sitting across the table from you for this trick. If they can see you from the side, they might catch sight of the sleight of hand in step 7.

4 NEXT WRAP THE GLASS TIGHTLY in the paper napkin. Make sure to form the napkin to the shape of the glass.

5 NOW ACT LIKE YOU'RE READY FOR THE TRICK. Close your eyes, mutter some "magic words," and lift the napkin-covered glass off the table.

6 OF COURSE, THE COIN HASN'T MOVED. Act embarrassed. Then try the trick two more times, each time getting angry at the coin for not cooperating.

7 NOW COMES THE TRICKY PART. After the last "failed" attempt, pick up the coin, hold it up in the air, and give it a good tongue lashing. As you're doing this, slide the napkin-covered glass to the edge of the table and let the glass fall down into your lap as you hold gently onto the napkin. Be sure not to squeeze too hard. You want the napkin to retain the shape of the glass.

⑦

8 WHEN YOU'RE DONE CURSING THE COIN, place it back on the table and put the glass-shaped napkin over the coin.

9 START YOUR MAGIC WORDS, but this time smash your hand down on top of the glass-shaped napkin so that it squashes down on the table. Be sure and slap your hand on the table to give the audience a startling bang.

10 AFTER A MOMENT OF CONFUSION, look under the napkin and let the audience know that you have made a solid pass through a solid after all. Reach into your lap and pull out the glass. It looks as though the glass has passed through the table!

The real trick here is what magicians call "misdirection"—keeping your audience's full attention on the coin, when actually you're performing the trick on the glass. Practice handling the hollow paper "glass" like the real thing, so you can convince your audience that the glass is still in there right up to the moment your hand bangs on the table.

Optical illusions

✦ ✦

An optical illusion is anything that isn't what it looks like. Magicians are experts at optical illusions because they can trick the brain into seeing something that isn't there. One of the most famous optical illusions performed by magicians is called the Balducci Levitation. Standing at an angle and facing away from the audience, a person lifts him or herself up on the ball of one foot. The audience can't see that area of the foot and it appears that the person is levitating a little way off the ground. Here are two more optical illusions you can try at home:

Magical photograph

One of the easiest illusions to achieve is the magical photograph. Here, you push objects into a flat piece of clay to make impressions. Then you take a picture. The photo should come out appearing as if the impressions are raised objects instead of indentations.

YOU WILL NEED

- Modeling clay
- A flat surface
- A rolling pin
- Various household objects like shells, coins, combs, etc.
- A digital camera
- A bright desk lamp

STEPS

1 ROLL THE CLAY OUT onto a flat surface.

2 COLLECT SMALL OBJECTS with easily recognizable contours, like keys, shells, coins, etc. Choose one and press it into the clay to leave an impression.

3 REMOVE THE OBJECT, turn on a bright lamp, and direct it straight down onto the impression in the clay. Photograph the imprint with your camera.

4 PRINT OUT THE PICTURE and turn it upside-down. The imprint in the photograph should appear to be a raised object!

Flip book

This optical illusion can turn lots of still images into a movie. That's what the old movie-makers did: their reel-to-reel film cameras essentially took lots of individual photographs so that when they were put side by side and sped up they took on the appearance of movement. A flip book does the same thing, but on paper.

YOU WILL NEED
- About 10 sheets of heavy-weight print paper
- A pair of scissors
- A pencil
- A stapler

STEPS

1 CUT THE PRINT PAPER INTO 50 PIECES that are 2 inches (5 cm) wide by 3 inches (7.5 cm) long. Stack the pieces together and staple one side to make a mini book.

2 USING A PENCIL, start at the back of the book and draw the action. You might want to try out by drawing a stick person first. He could be running or doing something more complicated. Get creative.

3 DRAW ONLY ON THE RIGHT-HAND SHEETS in the book. Alter your drawing slightly on each page so that it has a natural motion when you start to "flip" the pages.

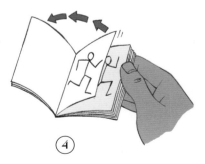

4 WHEN YOU'RE DONE, use your thumb to flip through the pages in rapid succession. The scene in the book should look like a movie.

The classics

There are some tricks that explorers have encountered in their travels for generations. These have been found in roadside carnivals and state fairs since our father's fathers were youngsters. And for good reason—they're fun and impressive! Unfortunately, these tricks aren't for us to duplicate at home. But knowing about the Bed of Nails, the Indian Rope Trick, the Bullet Catch, the Snake Charmer, and the Flea Circus is good information for any explorer to have.

Bed of Nails

The old Bed of Nails trick is a classic among classics. For centuries, various mystery-men and magicians have used this trick as their bread and butter. The idea is that the person performing the trick lies on a bed of nails and comes up unscathed. Sometimes an assistant places a concrete block on the magician's chest, and even smashes it with a sledgehammer, and still no blood is drawn.

The reason the trick works—and the reason the person laying on all those nails isn't impaled under his own weight—has to do with a simple rule of pressure. Pressure is the amount of weight in a given area. Scientists know that applying a weight over a small area (thus creating a high pressure) causes more damage than the same weight over a large area. When a magician lays down on a grid of nails, his weight is spread out over all the nails, making the pressure on each point relatively small. If there were only one nail, all his weight would push down on it and it would go right through him!

Indian Rope Trick

Because it's been around for at least 600 years and has been performed in so many different ways, no one's really sure if the Indian Rope Trick is real or just a legend. The trick involved a rope that a magician would throw up into the air, where it would magically stay erect. Then the magician's assistant would climb the rope—still held magically upright—and either climb down again or disappear up into the clouds and reappear somewhere else.

Another version takes on a pretty gruesome—and somewhat far-fetched—ending. It has the magician chasing up the rope after his assistant with a sword. There would be a scream, and then severed limbs would fall from up above—supposedly the remains of the assistant—after which the magician would descend, gather up the limbs, and have the assistant reappear alive from inside of a box. Okaaaaay. At least it gets your audience's attention.

DID YOU KNOW? Marco Polo has an account of a trick similar to the Indian Rope Trick in his travel log from the late thirteenth century.

The Bullet Catch

Another all-time great, the Bullet Catch creates the illusion that someone catches in their teeth a bullet fired at them from a gun. Many times, glass will be put between the magician and the gun so that it appears the bullet destroys the glass, proving that it really has been fired. The trick has been around since the late 1700s, and was very popular. One magician in the nineteenth century—a Scottish man named John Henry Anderson—performed the trick for Czar Nicholas of Russia and Queen Victoria of England.

Obviously no one can catch a bullet in their teeth. And no one should ever try to do so! So how does it work? There are several different techniques magicians use to perform the Bullet Catch. One uses a wax bullet in the gun instead of a real one. The magician loads the wax bullet into the gun in front of the audience so that it looks like he's putting a real bullet in. Then he slips a real bullet in his mouth, or he has put it there before the trick even begins. When his assistant fires the gun, the liquid from the melted wax shoots out the barrel and breaks the glass pane between the gun and the magician's mouth. The rest is just play-acting.

Snake charming

Snake charming also has its origins in India and it too has been around a long time. But unlike the Indian Rope Trick, it is still performed widely (at last count there were at least one million professional snake charmers on record in India). It's also a legitimate skill—there are no rubber snakes on wires or mechanized serpents here. They're all real.

Traditionally, the snake charmer carries his snake—usually a cobra—in a basket with a lid. When it's time for the performance, he puts the basket on the ground, removes the lid, and begins to play a tune on an Indian-style flute. As he plays, the snake pokes its head and part of its body out of the top of the basket. Then, as the tune goes on, the snake sways back and forth as if he's moving to the rhythm of the song. Some charmers even kiss the snakes at the end of the trick.

It all sounds do-able, right? Right. And it is. But the reason the snake comes out of its basket has nothing to do with the music. Snakes can't hear. Instead, snake charmers are experts on snake behavior. They are careful to sit just beyond the snake's striking range, which is about a distance equal to one third of the length of the snake's body. (Most charmers also carry snake bite kits with them because they do sometimes get bit, even though it's rare.)

The snake comes out of the basket when the charmer starts playing because he's curious. Having been in a dark basket, any animal is going to want to investigate the light when the lid is taken off. The charmer makes sure the snake is awake by waving his instrument over the top of the basket or tapping his foot (snakes can feel vibrations through the earth even though they can't hear). The swaying back and forth is the snake following the back-and-forth motion of the charmer's flute — similar to how it might follow the movement of its prey. As for kissing the snake — well, it is true that snakes can't strike things above them, but still don't try it at home. For the professionals, it helps to have that snake bite kit handy.

Flea circus

The flea circus trick is just that — a trick. Training fleas to see-saw, push a ball around, and ride a miniature Ferris wheel is simply impossible, and anyone who really spends their time trying has too much time on their hands. Or they're pulling your leg, which is how the trick usually works. To pull this one off, a magician needs a set of miniature, mechanically moving circus equipment. Perhaps even more important than that, he needs a flair for performance.

As the little contraptions are moving around the table under their own steam, it's up to him to convince everyone else that tiny fleas are actually powering the event. That said, it is possible to include fleas in the performance. Flea experts say that you can prevent fleas from jumping by keeping them in a jar for three days. Then all you have to do is place them on top of and in amongst the props to heighten your illusion.

Mexican jumping beans

With the Mexican Jumping Bean we're actually getting back to a little science rather than magic. Even though it seems that a bean that literally hops and jumps around is completely unnatural, the fact is it's just what Mother Nature intended. The only thing that is a little misleading is the word "bean." These little things are actually seeds that look like brown beans. They really are native to Mexico.

What's going on is that these seeds are the homes of moth caterpillars, or larvae. There is a type of small gray moth (called *Cydia deshaisiana*) that lays an egg in these seeds. When the egg hatches, the larva eats and hollows out the inside of the seed. Then it spins a silken thread to attach itself in the hollow, where it will live for several months before becoming a moth itself. The "beans" "jump" when the larvae inside them are slightly warmed—the heat from the palm of your hand is enough to do it. What happens is that the larva senses the heat and twitches and pulls at the silken thread around it, which makes the "bean" move around and hop. "Jump" is actually an exaggeration, but it is enough to make *you* jump if you're not expecting it.

WARNING

If you do get hold of some beans remember there's a live animal inside, so don't treat them too roughly. After all, if you hurt the larva in the nut, it won't be able to jump. Plus, if you look after your beans for a few weeks, there's a good chance you'll see them hatch out into moths (see page 53).

You can actually buy packets of Mexican Jumping Beans and use them as part of a magic show. Just don't plan a performance around springtime. The larva inside will eat a hole in the seed during the spring months and fly away as a moth!

Some people have even been known to race jumping beans by warming them a little so they get ready to hop, and putting them on a piece of card with a circle drawn on it. The beans all start at the center of the circle, and the first one to cross the line is the winner.

Making your own jumping beans

You can easily make your own jumping beans without having to find caterpillars using this method:

YOU WILL NEED

- Tin foil
- A marble about ¼ inch (6 mm) in diameter
- A pen a little wider than your marble
- A plastic box
- Sticky tape

STEPS

1 WRAP TIN FOIL AROUND YOUR PEN to make a small tube about 1 inch (2.5 cm) long, and wide enough for the marble to fit easily inside. Use enough foil to go round the pen three or four times, so the tube is good and sturdy. Use a bit of tape to hold the tube together.

2 TAKE THE PEN OUT OF THE TUBE carefully, so the foil retains its shape. Put the tube over your finger and mold one end so it's closed off.

3 SLIDE THE MARBLE DOWN THE TUBE and carefully mold the other end around it, so both ends of the tube are rounded off.

4 PUT YOUR ROUNDED TUBE IN A PLASTIC BOX and shake it from side to side so it rattles against the walls of the box. Keep it tilted away from you so only the ends hit the walls. This should mold the ends of the tube more closely to the marble.

5 NOW YOUR "BEAN" IS READY. Put it at the top of a slope and set it rolling down end-over-end. If you get it right it'll make the foil tube flip over as it rolls. If you spin it across a flat surface, it'll develop an unusual "wiggle" as it moves. Try out a few tricks, and see what you can do.

The ice hand

❖

Sometimes you need a spare hand. With this trick you can have one. It just won't be attached to your body! The ice hand is great for Halloween or other times you want to make people jump.

YOU WILL NEED

- An old rubber glove
- A large empty soda bottle
- A pair of scissors
- A knife
- 2 wooden skewers
- A measuring cup
- Water
- Food coloring
- A freezer

STEPS

1 USING SCISSORS, CUT OFF 3 INCHES (7.5 CM) from the bottom of the rubber dish glove so that only the hand, fingers, and a little of the wrist remain.

2 USING A KNIFE, cut off the top of the soda bottle so that the glove can hang down inside it without touching the bottom.

3 PUSH THE TWO WOODEN SKEWERS into the wrist of the glove to make an "X" and place the glove inside the soda bottle using the skewers for support.

4 MIX WATER AND FOOD COLORING inside a measuring cup. Then fill the rubber glove with the mixture.

5 PLACE THE GLOVE and its soda-bottle base in the freezer and wait until it freezes — about 5-8 hours.

6 REMOVE THE FROZEN HAND from the freezer and cut off the rubber glove with your scissors. *Voila!*

WARNING

Food coloring will stain carpets, clothes, furniture, and anything else it comes in contact with, so be careful with the frozen hand when it starts to melt.

The pre-sliced banana

The pre-sliced banana trick is very easy to do and always gets a great reaction. For those explorers wanting to give one of their friends or their little brother a surprise, this is a great trick to start with.

This is a very easy trick and you can prepare it in less than a minute. But despite being so easy it can create a big surprise, especially if the person you play it on isn't expecting it.

YOU WILL NEED

- A banana
- A needle
- A gullible friend

STEPS

1 ALL BANANAS HAVE RIDGES running down their outsides. Push a needle into one of these ridges near the top of the banana.

2 GENTLY MOVE THE NEEDLE to the left and right inside the banana so that you cut through the fruit but do not disturb the peel. Try to keep the needle hole as small as possible.

3 REPEAT THIS PROCESS in about six more spots along the length of the banana. Don't make the holes too close together, and always stick the needle into a ridge on the peel, where the hole will be less obvious. Remove the needle.

4 HAND THE BANANA to an unsuspecting brother, sister, or friend. Tell them you just learned a trick that enables you to slice a banana with the power of your mind. Spin them a yarn using your best magician's skills. Then watch as they peel the banana and get a big surprise!

Cup and ball tricks

✦

Here's a good, clean magic trick that's been making the magician's circuit for centuries. Like most good tricks it can be done quite simply but it has a big impact. What you'll do is seemingly pass paper balls magically through the end of a cup after stacking them all up together. You don't need any special skills or materials to perform this trick, and anyone who has about 30 minutes to practice should be able to pull it off.

YOU WILL NEED

● A paper napkin

● 3 opaque (that means not transparent) plastic cups

STEPS

1 TEAR THE NAPKIN INTO FOUR EQUAL-SIZED PIECES and screw them up into four small paper balls.

2 SECRETLY PUT ONE OF THOSE PAPER BALLS inside a plastic cup and turn the cup over on the table with the ball underneath. Don't let anyone see you do this.

3 TURN THE TWO REMAINING CUPS UPSIDE DOWN on either side of that cup and lay out the remaining three balls in plain sight in front of the cups.

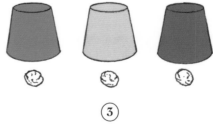

4 START THE TRICK by placing one of those three balls on top of the middle cup (the one with the secret ball under it). Tell your audience that you are going to make the ball pass by magic through the bottom of the cup and land on the table top.

5 **THEN STACK THE OTHER TWO CUPS** over the ball. When all three cups are stacked, say a few magic words and tap the top of the stack.

6 **LIFT THE STACK UP** to reveal the ball underneath — it looks as though the ball you put inside has magically passed through the cup.

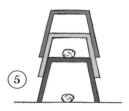

7 **CONTINUE BY REMOVING THE CUPS** and placing them upside down on the table.

8 **AS YOU REMOVE THE SECOND CUP,** remember that there is a ball under it that your audience doesn't know about. Let the ball slide into the second cup as you take it off the stack — you can pretend that the cups are stuck together to cover for this. Then turn this cup over quickly so that the ball doesn't fall out.

9 **MAKE THIS CUP THE MIDDLE CUP** and put it down on top of the first ball you "magically" made appear. Now there should be two balls under the cup though everyone will think there's only one.

10 **NOW YOU CAN DO THE WHOLE THING AGAIN:** place one of the remaining balls on top of the middle cup (the one with the two secret balls under it), then place another ball on top of the middle cup and put the third cup on top.

11 **WHEN ALL THREE CUPS ARE STACKED,** say a few magic words and tap the top of the stack.

12 **LIFT THE STACK UP** to reveal two balls underneath — again, it looks as though the ball you put inside has magically passed through the cup. Lift up the second cup to show that the ball still there.

13 **REPEAT THE PROCESS A THIRD TIME** and all three balls will appear under the cup. Stack all the cups up together on top of the balls, so the secret fourth ball stays hidden, and take a bow.

Number tricks

✦ ✦

Number tricks will confuse and amaze everyone — even, at times, the magician himself. The good news is you don't have to be particularly good at math to do them. As long as you follow the directions, these tricks will add up! Before performing them, grab a calculator and try out a few on your own so you can see exactly how they work. That way you won't be caught, mid-performance, trying to remember what comes next.

Mind reading

You might not think it by looking at the numbers below, but this works every time. Try it on your own first. You'll amaze yourself the first time around and your friends will think you're a true mind reader. Either that or a math expert.

YOU WILL NEED
- A calculator
- A willing participant

STEPS

1 HAVE YOUR FRIEND THINK OF A NUMBER between 10 and 100. Tell them to keep it a secret — you'll uncover it soon enough.

2 NEXT, ASK THEM THEIR AGE and make a note of that number.

3 NOW COMES THE MATH. Use a calculator and do the following: Take their age, multiply it by 2, add 5 to that number, multiply the result by 50, and then subtract 365.

4 HAND THE CALCULATOR TO YOUR FRIEND and ask them to add their secret number to the number on the calculator and hand you back the calculator.

5 **WHEN YOU GET IT BACK,** add 115 to the number. You should end up with a three or four digit number (depending on how old the volunteer is.)

6 **THE END TWO NUMBERS** on the calculator are your volunteer's secret number. The first one or two numbers are their age.

Gray Elephant from Denmark

This trick won't necessarily work in a performance—it's really just something that's neat to figure out. The nice part is, you don't have to do any math—the other person does all the work, but you're the one who comes out looking smart. It's a great way to impress people who think they're better at math than you.

YOU WILL NEED

● A calculator   ● A volunteer

STEPS

1 **HAVE YOUR VOLUNTEER PICK A NUMBER** between 1 and 9, without telling you what it is.

2 **GIVE HIM THE CALCULATOR,** and tell him to subtract 5 from that number, again without telling you the result.

3 **TELL HIM TO MULTIPLY** the result by 3.

4 **GET HIM TO SQUARE** the result from step 3 (in other words, multiply the number by itself).

5 **NOW HE MUST ADD THE DIGITS** of the answer together—for example, if the number is 144 then add 1+4+4 to get 9.

6 **IF THE RESULTING NUMBER** is less than 5, get him to add 5. Otherwise he should subtract 4.

7 **TELL HIM TO MULTIPLY** by 2 (and tell him you're nearly finished . . .)

8 NOW TELL HIM TO SUBTRACT 6. The number he ends up with should always be 4—he doesn't know you know this, so you can use it to perform the rest of the trick.

9 TELL YOUR VOLUNTEER that you're going to assign a letter to his number and explain—quite reasonably—that the number will get a letter corresponding to its place in the alphabet, so: A=1, B=2, C=3, D=4, E=5, etc. Secretly, you know the number must be 4, so the letter must be D.

10 NEXT, ASK YOUR VOLUNTEER to pick a country (but not to tell you which one) that begins with the letter assigned to his number. There aren't many countries that start with the letter D. The most obvious one is Denmark. If he picks Dominican Republic, then you're out of luck.

11 THEN ASK HIM TO PICK AN ANIMAL that begins with the second letter from the country he picked. The second letter of Denmark is "E," and most people will say that an animal that starts with the letter "E" is "elephant." (What else would they choose? Emu?)

12 FINALLY, ASK HIM TO THINK of the color of that animal. Elephants are always gray.

13 TELL HIM HE'S THINKING of a gray elephant from Denmark, and watch his jaw drop!

The trick here is in step 5. No matter which number you choose you will always end up with a number whose digits add up to either 9 or 0. That means that subtracting 5 or adding 4 will always get you 4 and the corresponding letter "D." Chances are everyone will choose Denmark and elephant. It's not foolproof but the odds are in your favor.

You can make more of the trick by drawing out the final step. Close your eyes and wave a hand in front of his face, saying, "I can see a letter . . . it looks like . . . a D! Denmark! Your country's Denmark! And I can see an animal . . . very large . . . with big ears . . ." Make a performance out of it to increase the trick's impact.

Card trick

❖

No chapter on tricking would be complete without a quick card trick—the favorite tool in any magician's kit. Card tricks are great because you don't need a lot of complicated equipment or preparation—that's probably why they're so popular amongst magicians all over the world.

Here's one that's easy to do, but guaranteed to impress anybody you show it to. Like all magic, the real trick here is very simple, and it's up to you to disguise it—and keep your audience entertained—with as much showmanship as possible.

YOU WILL NEED
- A pack of playing cards
- A volunteer

STEPS

1 SHUFFLE THE CARDS THOROUGHLY, then fan them out and let your volunteer pick one. Tell them to remember what it is, but not to show it to you.

2 TELL THEM TO SHOW IT TO THE AUDIENCE as well, so everybody except you can see. While they're doing this, and the audience's attention is distracted, take a look at the bottom card of the pack and remember it.

3 TELL YOUR VOLUNTEER to put their card back on top of the pack. Then cut the pack, putting the bottom half on the top. Your volunteer's card will now be right next to the card you've memorized from the bottom of the deck.

4 YOU CAN CUT THE DECK a couple more times to make it look as though you're mixing the cards up, but don't shuffle them.

5 WHEN YOU FEEL YOU'VE MIXED THINGS up enough, turn the pack over and sort through looking for the card you memorized from the bottom of the pack. When you find it, pick out the one before and show it to your audience. Ta-da!

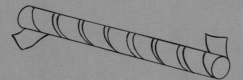

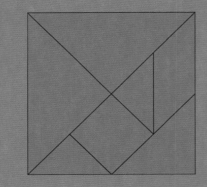

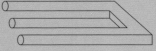

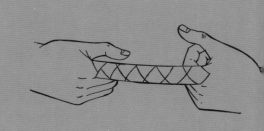

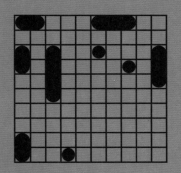

Chapter Five

Puzzling

IF YOU'RE A TRUE EXPLORER
you can never pass up a good brain twister, logic
puzzle, or number game. Just like they can't resist
tinkering with a room full of chemistry
experiments, explorers will take any opportunity
to test their brainpower.

✦

In this chapter, prepare to stretch your mental
muscles by deciphering codes and solving clues.
And keep an eye on the time—some of these games
can cause a whole afternoon to disappear before
you can say "Game On!"

Codes and ciphers

❖❖

The practice of altering words and substituting letters to make secret codes has been around for thousands of years. By scrambling up their words and letters, members of armies and secret societies can communicate with each other without worrying about the message falling into enemy hands. If it did, the enemy wouldn't be able to read it because they wouldn't know how to break the code. Only the people sending and receiving the message know the key.

Of course, as long as there have been codes, there have been people trying to crack them—explorers included. Code-makers and code-breakers have been in a secret battle for thousands of years. New codes appear all the time—they're used until people figure out how to crack them, and then replaced with even more complicated puzzles.

Today, computers allow us to create incredibly complex methods for sharing information in secret, and most old-fashioned codes have been replaced by ciphers. Ciphers are different than codes in that they use highly complex algorithms— mathematical equations often operated by computers—to create coded messages that are very difficult to break. They're often used to protect information transmitted over the Internet, to keep your personal details private when you buy something, for example.

Still, cracking an ordinary code is good fun, and using secret messages can be a great way to communicate with your friends and other explorers, without letting anyone else in on your secrets. Start with some basic codes and work your way up. Creating your own codes for you and your friends is half the fun—and that way you can be sure nobody else knows how to crack them. Here are a few you can use to get you started. It always helps to write up a code book with the letters of the alphabet written in a column on the left and their corresponding code letter or symbol in a column on the right.

Codewords and phrases

Perhaps the simplest codes are random phrases and passwords that only you and your friends know. Secret agents used these passwords—which could be as simple as "The sun is shining"—when they were meeting contacts for the first time. If your contact didn't respond with the correct phrase—for example, "But it might rain later"—you could tell they weren't who they said they were. The problem is that these codes can only be used for pre-set messages, and once the enemy has worked out what they mean, you can't use them again.

Substitution codes

The next simplest type of code is called a "simple substitution," where each letter is replaced by another letter or symbol. For example, this could mean substituting the letter you intend with the next letter of the alphabet, so if you really mean to write "A" use a "B." An "M" in code would be a "N" and so on. For the letter "Z" use "A." You can use these for extended written messages.

Using this code, the word "ENEMY" would be written as "FOFNZ." You can make things more complicated by skipping two or even three letters, so "A" becomes "C" or "D," and "ENEMY" becomes "GPGOA" or "HQHPB."

If you think this code might still be too easy to break, try making things more complicated. Allow the vowels to remain their real letter and change only consonants. Shift different letters on different lines, so "A" is "B" on line 1, but "C" on line 2. There are many variations, including substituting numbers for certain letters, or replacing the whole alphabet with your own set of symbols and pictograms.

The only problem with these codes is that they are easy for an experienced code-breaker to crack using "frequency analysis." Because certain letters appear more regularly in the English language than others, you can count up which symbols in a coded message appear most frequently and work out which letters they must be. For example, the letter "E" comes up more frequently in English than any other letter, so the most common symbol in your coded message probably stands for "E." (Sherlock Holmes uses this method to solve a mysterious and deadly code in the story "The Adventure of the Dancing Men.")

DID YOU KNOW? During World War II, the German armed forces used a machine codenamed "Enigma" to create coded messages. The code worked by susbtitution, but the machine used rotors that switched the substituted letters around as the message was sent, making it very difficult to break. Allied mathematicians and codebreakers at Bletchley Park in England eventually cracked the code using their own machine, allowing them to spy on German attack plans in secret.

The scytale

This was a method of code-writing used by the Ancient Greeks. It requires you and the person receiving your message each to have a piece of dowel of exactly the same diameter. It works not by changing the letters of the code around, but by concealing which letters are part of the message and which are red herrings.

YOU WILL NEED
- A pencil
- Two identical pieces of dowel
- A strip of paper

STEPS

1 CUT A THIN STRIP OF PAPER and wrap it around your piece of dowel.

2 WRITE YOUR MESSAGE along the dowel so one letter goes on each turn of the paper.

3 UNWRAP THE PAPER, and you should see the letters of your message jumbled across the strip.

4 ADD OTHER LETTERS around them so your message is concealed, and anybody looking at the strip just sees jumbled nonsense.

5 SEND THE PIECE OF PAPER TO YOUR CONTACT. When they wrap it round their piece of dowel, the letters of your original message will rearrange themselves in order.

The Ancient Greeks seem to have been very interested in secret writing. They invented lots of other techniques, including hiding messages under layers of wax on a writing tablet, and even tattooing them onto the messenger's shaved scalp, so that the message would be hidden under a new growth of hair.

Crosswords

✦✦✦

Crosswords are word puzzles that fit into a grid. The goal is to solve the clues given to you and then write the answers into the grid. You can then use the letters of these words to help you guess the other words in the puzzle.

Crossword puzzles were invented in New York in 1913 by a man named Arthur Wynne. Since then the game has become hugely popular. In fact, some people say that crossword puzzles are the most popular game in the world. They exist in almost every language on the planet and are published in nearly every newspaper. There are dozens of books, websites, and crossword clubs devoted to them and how to solve them.

Tips on solving crosswords

The tricky part, of course, is that the people who set the clues always do their best to hide the answers from you. They do this by phrasing them in a misleading manner, sometimes even turning them into mini-riddles for you to try to untangle.

The good news is, there are loads of tricks and tips to help you solve crossword puzzles, and the more you do them the more you will become familiar with different types of clues. Here are a few tips to get you started:

TIPS

1 EVERY CLUE HAS A NUMBER, and the answer goes in the boxes on the grid that start with that number. The boxes go across and down the page, so the clues are divided into "across" and "down." Every clue has another number after it in brackets—that's the number of letters in the answer. Easy so far, right?

2 THERE ARE TWO TYPES OF CROSSWORD CLUES: "straight" and "cryptic." Straight clues usually just require you to think of a synonym (a word that means the same) for the clue word. For example, the straight clue "Boat (4)" might have the answer "ship."

3 CRYPTIC CLUES ARE TRICKIER, because they rely more on thinking outside the box. Sometimes you have to think of other meanings words might have, and

that meaning is never the obvious one—these clues are always written so as to put you off the scent.

4 CRYPTIC CLUES ALWAYS HAVE A STRAIGHT CLUE built into them, as well as a lateral-thinking clue. The difficult part is working out which one's which! If you're not getting anywhere trying to solve one half of a clue, try looking at the other half to see if that makes the answer any clearer.

5 CROSSWORD ANSWERS ALWAYS AGREE in tense and number with their clues. For example, if the clue is in the past tense—"Performed a song (4)"—then the answer will be in the past tense—"sang" not "sing." If a clue is plural, the answer will be plural—"Flying creatures (4)" may be "bats" but not "bird."

6 START WITH "FILL-IN-THE-BLANK" CLUES, because they're usually the easiest. (For example, "Mary had a little ＿＿＿ (4)" The answer is obviously "lamb.") Then you can use the letters from those answers to help you out with the harder clues.

7 IF A CLUE USES AN ABBREVIATION, or if the word "abbr." is in the clue, then the answer is going to be abbreviated. (So "United States of America abbr. (3)" will be "USA."

8 IF A CLUE HAS THE WORD "ANAG." in it, it means the answer is an anagram—a word made by jumbling up the letters of other words in the clue. So "Heart anag. (5)" might be "earth." In cryptic clues, anagrams are often indicated with words like "mixed up" or "confused," telling you to mix up the letters. So the same clue in cryptic form might be, "Heart troubled for our planet (5)"—"Heart troubled" means mix up the letters in "heart," and the name of our planet is of course "Earth."

9 A LOT OF CROSSWORD CLUES USE THE WORD "POINT," which means the answer is going to include an abbreviation of one of the points of a compass, N, E, S, or W. Other words with special meaning include "ship" (usually SS), "river" (R), and "time" (T). A clue might be "At two points by a river it's time for a sit-down (4)." The two points are E and S (east and south), the river is R, time is T, and a sit-down is a REST. (And you might need one after puzzling all that out!)

Finger cuffs

The trick with finger traps—which are sometimes called "Chinese handcuffs," or "finger cuffs"—has less to do with playing a game and more to do with trying to escape. A quick look at this puzzle—made of tough bamboo or grass woven together into a cylinder—doesn't reveal anything about its trapping technique. Only when you put your two index fingers in each end and then try to pull them out do you realize the mess you've gotten yourself into. The finger cuffs get tighter the harder you pull. You're stuck!

The material these traps are made of is nothing special—try hard enough and you could probably tear it, though that still wouldn't get it off your fingers. The trick has to do with the braid. Known as a biaxial braid, this weave naturally gets smaller as you pull on it. And of course the natural inclination of anyone who puts their fingers inside a tube is to remove them by pulling them straight out. That doesn't work here.

To escape, you have to go against your instinct and push your fingers together. That widens the braided opening. Then all you have to do is either slowly twist your fingers out, or hold the cuffs with your thumb and middle finger while pulling your index finger out.

Once you do figure out how to get your fingers free from the cuffs, get a friend to put them on, and then watch as he struggles to get his fingers out. That's when the fun really begins.

Riddles

✤ ✤

If you find yourself stuck in a car for a long summer road trip, and you've exhausted all the crossword puzzles, hand-held video games, and books, you can always have fun with word games. Riddles are a type of word game where a statement or question has to be figured out, like a puzzle to be solved.

There's more to it than just general knowledge tests, though, where the answer is a straight fact—riddles use double meanings that the listener has to unveil in order to get to the answer, like the tougher crossword clues. Some of them require a knowledge of history, while others use puns to play on the sounds of words. Either way, the answer can only come after some careful thought and an equally playful response.

Here are a few riddles to play with:

What creature walks on four legs in the morning, on two legs in the afternoon, and on three legs in the evening?
Answer: A human. In the first part of life (the morning) a baby crawls around on all fours; in the middle of life (afternoon) we walk on two legs; and at the end of life (evening) we walk with a cane, which added to our two other legs makes three. This riddle was told by the Sphinx to the hero Oedipus in Greek mythology. He got it right, thankfully—the monster threatened to eat him if he didn't!

What relation would your father's sister's sister-in-law be to you?
Answer: Your mother. This riddle works by making the question sound more complicated than it really is.

Can you name three consecutive days of the week without using the words Monday, Tuesday, Wednesday, Thursday, Friday, Saturday, or Sunday?
Answer: Yesterday, today, and tomorrow.

If a red house is made of red bricks and a yellow house is made of yellow bricks what's a greenhouse made of?
Answer: Glass.

There is an ancient invention still used in many parts of the world today that allows people to see through walls. What is it?
Answer: A window.

I know a word of letters three. Add two, and fewer there will be.
Answer: The word "few."

What gets wetter the more it dries?
Answer: A towel.

What goes up when the rain comes down?
Answer: An umbrella.

Making your own riddles

One way to make your own riddles is to think about other meanings that words might have—that'll help with your crosswords, too. An example might be: "I'm as light as a feather, but you can't hold me for long. What am I?" The answer is "breath," because the word "hold" can have different meanings.

Another way is to come up with a way of describing something that sounds more complicated than it really is. For example: "How can I write your exact weight on a piece of paper without weighing you?" The answer is to write the words "your exact weight" on a piece of paper and give it to them—much simpler than they were expecting!

Make up some riddles for yourself and try them out on your friends. Remember, the right answer should always be a lot simpler than the question makes out—the real aim of a riddle is to have everybody groaning when you tell them what it means!

DID YOU KNOW? Riddles have been around for thousands of years. They were very important in Norse (Anglo-Saxon and Viking) culture, where quick-witted bards (musicians and story-tellers) in mythology used them to outwit fierce warriors. J.R.R. Tolkien, the author of *The Lord of the Rings*, was very interested in Norse riddles, and they play an important part in his stories.

Tangrams

❖

Normally when we think of puzzles we think of hundreds of jigsaw pieces that fit together to form a picture (see page 88). Tangrams are a special type of jigsaw with only seven pieces, known as "tans," which have to fit next to each other without overlapping to form the shape of a person, animal, or object. The seven pieces are always the same — they are five right-angled isosceles triangles in three different sizes, one square, and one parallelogram.

Tangrams were invented in China hundreds of years ago and brought to Europe in the nineteenth century during a boom in trade with the Far East. In the past, people have made tangram pieces out of ivory, bone, clay, and wood. You can make your own set using thick cardboard.

YOU WILL NEED

- A square of cardboard at least 8 inches (20 cm) on each side
- A utility knife
- A ruler
- A pencil
- Paints

STEPS

1 CUT OUT A SQUARE of cardboard 8 inches (20 cm) on each side.

2 USING A RULER TO MEASURE the spacing, lightly draw a grid of squares 2 inches (5 cm) tall and wide on your cardboard. You should have 16 identical squares mapped out.

3 DRAW A DARK PENCIL LINE right across the cardboard square from corner to corner to make two large triangles.

4 DRAW A DARK PENCIL LINE from a third corner to cut one of the triangles in half.

5 DRAW DARK PENCIL LINES across the other large triangle to divide it into the remaining shapes as shown on the diagram.

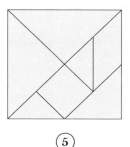

(5)

6 CUT OUT EACH PIECE, using a utility knife rather than scissors to retain the exact shapes. The seven pieces are your seven tans.

7 PAINT YOUR TANS in a single color of your choice—black is traditional, so your puzzles come out as silhouettes. When they're dry, you're ready to put some tangrams together.

There are hundreds of tangrams you can create with these seven tans, including animals, birds, letters of the alphabet, people, famous monuments . . . the list goes on. See if you can use your tans to make the designs below, then try inventing your own designs. Remember, the rules are: you must use all seven tans, they must all lay flat, and none of them can overlap.

Logic grids

✦✦

Logic grids are games often found in puzzle magazines, in which the player must use deductive logic to match up a series of categories. You're given groups of three, four, or five items, and clues that match up each item to one item in each other group. The trick is working out what links to what. These are fun. You get wrapped up in these and the time passes quickly.

Here's a nice, easy example to show you how these work. In this case, there are only three groups, and each group has only three items in it.

The puzzle

Lancelot has been given a quest to kill three dragons: one red, one green, and one black. He met three wizards—Merlin, Mordred, and Taliesin—who each gave him a magic spear: one gold, one silver, and one bronze. Each spear has been made to kill one specific dragon, but Lancelot can't remember which one's which.

1. Lancelot remembers that Merlin gave him a spear to kill the red dragon, but that the spear was not gold.
2. Taliesin's spear wasn't meant to kill the black dragon, and it is not gold.
3. The green dragon is invulnerable to the bronze spear.

How to solve the puzzle

1 THE WAY TO SOLVE THESE is to mark out what you already know from the clues in the grid that comes with the puzzle. In this case, the grid for this puzzle would look like this. Each square represents a relationship between two elements of the puzzle. For example, the top-left box here shows whether Merlin told Launcelot how to kill the red dragon.

	red	green	black	gold	silver	bronze
Merlin						
Mordred						
Taliesin						
gold						
silver						
bronze						

2 WE KNOW FROM THE FIRST CLUE that he did, so we can put a tick in that box. And we can put "X"s against the red dragon for the other wizards (since each wizard knew how to kill only one dragon), and against Merlin for the other dragons. We also know that this spear wasn't gold, so we can put an "X" in the box that links Merlin with the gold spear, and (because Merlin and the red dragon are connected) the box linking the red dragon and the gold spear.

	red	green	black	gold	silver	bronze
Merlin	✓	✗	✗	✗		
Mordred	✗					
Taliesin	✗					
gold	✗					
silver						
bronze						

3 CLUE TWO TELLS US TO CROSS OUT THE SQUARES connecting Taliesin and the black dragon, and Taliesin and the gold spear. We know Taliesin couldn't have told Lancelot about the red dragon, because Merlin did, so Taliesin must have advised on the green dragon, which means Mordred must have talked about the black one. We also know that neither Merlin nor Taliesin gave Lancelot the gold spear, so Mordred must have done. Which means the gold spear must be used to kill the black dragon. Our grid is nearly complete.

	red	green	black	gold	silver	bronze
Merlin	✓	✗	✗	✗		
Mordred	✗	✗	✓	✓	✗	✗
Taliesin	✗	✓	✗	✗		
gold	✗	✗	✓			
silver		✗				
bronze		✗				

4 FINALLY, WE KNOW FROM CLUE THREE that the bronze spear won't harm the green dragon, and since the gold spear only works against the black dragon, the silver spear must be for the green dragon and the bronze spear for the red. Since Merlin knew how to kill the red dragon, he must have given Lancelot the bronze spear, and the silver one must have come from Taliesin. We can fill in the last squares, and the puzzle is solved.

	red	green	black	gold	silver	bronze
Merlin	✓	✗	✗	✗	✗	✓
Mordred	✗	✗	✓	✓	✗	✗
Taliesin	✗	✓	✗	✗	✓	✗
gold	✗	✗	✓			
silver	✗	✓	✗			
bronze	✓	✗	✗			

Sudoku

✠✠✠

The king of logic grid puzzles is a number game called Sudoku.
It was invented in the United States in 1979 as a game called
"Number Place," but only became really popular a few years later
in Japan. That's where it got the name Sudoku. Now you find it
everywhere—in newspapers, magazines, and on the Internet.

To play, you don't have to know algebra or even how to add 2 + 2. All you have to
do is to count from 1 to 9. The trick of the puzzle is figuring out where to place the
numbers. The rules are these: you have to fill a grid nine squares by nine, so that
each column, each row, and each of the nine three-by-three boxes contains the
digits from 1 to 9 without repeating any of the numbers. Each puzzle comes with
some of the squares filled in—like clues in a crossword puzzle.

At first glance, this may seem tough if not impossible. But there are some
strategies you can use to complete the grid.

Strategies

1 THE FIRST STRATEGY and the easiest one to master is called cross-hatching. By
looking along rows and down columns and within each 3 x 3 section, you can
often determine where a number is supposed to go and where it isn't supposed
to go. Here, we've used cross-hatching to find out where the 7 goes in the top-

right section (C). We know that neither of the two columns highlighted in red can have another 7, and neither can the top row. Because the middle-right square has a 3 in it, only the bottom-right square of section C can hold the 7. Once you start filling in the boxes with numbers, continue to cross-hatch into other sections using the new numbers you've just found.

2 AFTER YOU'VE FILLED IN AS MANY BOXES as possible by cross-hatching, you can then begin to determine what numbers might go in the remaining squares. Usually you can narrow the number down to two or three possibilities by looking along the row and column, and around the rest of the square, and seeing what's left over. Use a pencil and lightly write in those possibilities in tiny numbers in one corner of the square. Try to do this only when you have narrowed down to two or three possibilities, otherwise your grid is just going to be a mess. Here, for example, only 3, 4, and 7 are left to go in the top-middle section of the grid (B), so we can write 3, 4, and 7 in small in each box.

3 ONCE YOU'VE OUTLINED THE POSSIBILITIES, you can go back to cross-hatching and see what you find out. In this case, cross-hatching tells us that the 3 must go in the top-left corner of section B, because the 3 in the center of section E means that no other 3s can go in that column.

WARNING

Always make your marks in pencil, because you can be sure you'll need to erase your numbers at least once.

More logic puzzles

There are plenty of other logic puzzles out there to tax your brain cells. Here are a couple more to keep you amused when logic grids and Sudoku are threatening to drive you crazy.

Knights and Knaves

The logic game known as Knights and Knaves presents statements that you have to decipher. Essentially, the game takes place on a make-believe island where there are only two types of people: knights and knaves. Knights always tell the truth and knaves always lie, but there's no other way to tell which is which. The game is set up with statements from the inhabitants of the island, and it's your job to use logic to try and figure out who is a knight and who is a knave. Here's a puzzle and its answer, based on formal logic:

You're walking down the beach of the island of Knights and Knaves and you run into two fellows, John and Bill. John says: "We are both knaves." Who is who?

Answer: To get to the bottom of this you have to use formal logic. Start by breaking down the question. Instead of John saying "we are both knaves" he could also say "John is a knave and Bill is a knave." Now, if John were a knight he could not lie and say he was a knave. Therefore, we have to assume that John is in fact a knave. But what about Bill? Since John is a knave (as we've already determined) and he's the one doing the talking then all his statements must be false. Therefore, since John said "Bill is a knave" we know that to be false. Bill is in fact a knight.

Battleships

If you haven't heard of this game, ask your dad—or your granddad. Both ought to know it either as a board game or a pencil and paper game from years ago. The board game was more of a guessing game, in which two players tried to guess where each other's ships were located on a large grid. Battleship puzzles, found in puzzle magazines, are a little different. They're for one player, and you're still trying to locate "ships" but there's no guessing about it—you use logic to find them.

Essentially, battleship puzzles are grids with 10 squares on each side, with numbers on the right and bottom sides. The numbers are the clues. They let you know how many squares in each row and column must be occupied by a "ship."

The object of the game is to find the locations of the 10 ships in the puzzle. Each puzzle will contain exactly one battleship (which takes up four squares), two cruisers (three squares each), three destroyers (two squares each), and four submarines (one sqare each). It's your job to draw in the ships and submarines. The ships may be oriented either horizontally or vertically in the grid. However, no two ships may touch, even diagonally. That means each ship will be completely surrounded by water, which you should draw in as well. Most of the time a battleship puzzle will start out with a few clues or "reveals" to get you started. Remember, use the numbers on the right and bottom as clues to how many ship segments must appear in that row or column.

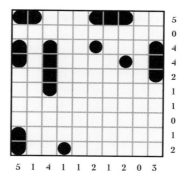

STRATEGY:

1 AS YOU START EACH GAME, fill in what you know in squares adjacent to what has already been revealed in the puzzle. For example, if a submarine has been revealed in a hint, you can label all the squares around it as water.

2 NEXT, FILL IN ANY WATER in the rows and columns that have all the ship segments already in place. If a row or column has the number zero next to it, for example, you can instantly label all its squares as water. If it has a one, and the hints have already shown you one segment, the rest of the squares will be water.

3 FINALLY, TRY TO MATCH SHIP SEGMENTS in the remaining rows and columns with the corresponding number on the right or bottom of the grid. Remember that ships must always have at least one square of clear water between them.

Solitaire

✦ ✦

Here's a riddle: what's a game you can play alone, with kings and queens, and a lot of patience? The answer: Solitaire! This one-person card game is also known as Patience in Britain.

The goal is to play all 52 cards in a deck from the table onto winning piles by placing them in order by rank from the Ace to the King in four columns. The trick, however, is that you always have to play black on red and red on black, building up long chains of cards from King down to Two alternating between red and black colors. Most of the time, winning is down to the luck of the draw.

Rules of the game

There are hundreds of variations on the rules of solitaire, but the classic set-up goes like this:

YOU WILL NEED
- A deck of 52 cards (with no Jokers)
- A table
- Patience

SETTING UP

1 SHUFFLE THE DECK, and deal out seven cards side by side on the table top. Turn the card farthest to the left face up while leaving the other six face down.

2 DEAL OUT SIX MORE CARDS on top of the six face-down cards. Again, turn the left-most card face up.

3 KEEP DEALING OUT CARDS IN THIS WAY, always turning the left-most card face up, and only dealing new cards onto the face-down piles. You should be left with seven piles, with one, two, three, four, five, six, and seven cards in them, and the top card on each pile face up.

4 ONCE YOU HAVE FACE-UP CARDS on each of the seven piles you should be left with a deck of 28 cards in your hand. Now you're ready to play

How to play

1 THE GOAL IS TO MOVE ALL THE CARDS out of the game by stacking them up in order by suit, starting with the Aces. To win, you need four neat piles of Spades, Hearts, Diamonds, and Clubs, each one running from Ace (which counts as number 1) up to King.

2 YOU CAN MOVE CARDS AROUND on the seven stacks by placing them on top of a card of the next highest rank and the opposite color: a red Ten can go on a black Jack, a black Five on a red Six, and so on.

3 START BY TRYING TO PLAY THE CARDS on the table top, taking any Aces out to start the winning piles, and stacking up any red-black or black-red sequences you can see. You may only make a play with face-up cards. Every time you move a card off a stack of down-turned cards, turn over the card underneath.

4 YOU CAN ALSO MOVE STACKS OF CARDS around on the table top. If you have a black Three on a red Four, and a black Five comes into play, you can move both the Three and Four onto the Five.

5 WHEN YOU GET STUCK, TAKE THREE CARDS off the top of the left-over deck and turn them over. Try to play the top one onto one of the stacks. If it goes, you can try to play the next card in your hand after that one, or see if more cards can now be played on the stacks.

6 IF YOU CAN'T PLAY THE TOP CARD in the set of three, you cannot play the cards under it. Place them as a group face up in a "discard pile" and draw three more cards off the deck to keep playing.

7 GO ALL THE WAY THROUGH the deck in this manner and then pick up the discard pile and go through it again, three cards at a time. If you get to the end of the deck and can't play a single card, then you may go through the deck one card at a time (but once only).

8 IF A COLUMN BECOMES EMPTY you can play a King in that empty space. However, you can never have more than seven columns.

9 TO WIN AT SOLITAIRE you must have all the table cards turned up and be able to play all the cards in the deck.

Clock solitaire

❖

Another solo card game is called Clock Solitaire (or Clock Patience), because you lay the cards out in a circle like numbers on a clock-face, and then try to match the cards with the numbers of the clock from one to 12.

Jacks represent the number 11, Queens the number 12, and Aces are number one. Kings are part of the game, but drawing them is not good. Here's how to play:

YOU WILL NEED
- A deck of 52 cards (with no Jokers)
- A table
- Patience

STEPS

1 TAKE ONE DECK OF CARDS—minus the Jokers—and deal them all out face down into 12 piles in a circle. Each pile should have four cards in it. The remaining four cards go face down in the middle of the circle.

2 START BY DRAWING THE TOP CARD OFF the middle pile and placing it face up under the deck of cards on its corresponding number (Aces go at one o'clock, Twos at two o'clock, and so on up to Queens at 12).

3 ONCE YOU PLACE THAT FIRST CARD, then you can turn over the top card of the deck you put it under. When that card is revealed, place it face up under the pile for its number and turn over the top of that pile, and so on.

4 IF A KING IS DRAWN IT GOES FACE UP under the central pile. When all four Kings are drawn the game is over.

5 YOU WIN IF YOU CAN REVEAL ALL THE OTHER CARDS on the clock face before all four Kings are drawn.

Rebuses

✦ ✦

Rebus puzzles are sometimes called pictogram puzzles because they use symbols, oddly placed words, and pictograms to get a message across. To read the message, you have to decipher what all the symbols, pictograms, and words mean.

There are a few different types of rebus techniques and one or all of them may be used in the same puzzle. Sometimes the pictograms in a rebus puzzle can be used for how they sound rather than what they mean. For example, to write the sentence "I see you" using the rebus principle, you might draw an eye (for "I"), a pictogram of the sea ("see"), and the shape of a female sheep or ewe ("you").

A rebus can also be used to form parts of a words. For example, "H" and a picture of an ear can be used to mean the word "hear" or "here."

Symbols can also be used to portray a message based on the meaning behind them. A famous rebus is "I heart NY," which means "I love New York."

In other rebus puzzles, words are used but they are arranged in suggestive ways. For example, one rebus puzzle uses the word "secret" written three times, one on top of the other, with an asterisk marking the "secret" at the top of the pile. Using the rebus principle, this message spells out "top secret."

Secret *
Secret
Secret

Other rebus puzzles use words spelled backward or placed in odd positions next to each other. In a rebus puzzle, the word "order" written in really tall letters means "tall order."

See if you can work this one out (the answer is over the page):

n
o
t
t
u   your
b   coat

The answer is: "button up your overcoat"—the word "button" is written upward, and "your" is over "coat."

Making your own

If you like the idea of making up your own rebus puzzles to try out on your friends, here are a few tips.

YOU WILL NEED
- A pen or pencil
- Paper
- Your imagination

STEPS

1 **THINK OF A FEW COMMON PHRASES** that everyone's heard of. You want your answer to be easy to recognize, so people will know it when they've got it. (It's no good having a puzzle where the answer is nonsense, because nobody will ever be able to work it out.)

2 **WRITE THE PHRASES DOWN AND THINK** about each of the words in turn. Are other ways you could represent them? For example, with any phrase with a color in it, you can just color one of the words next to it (so the phrase "red herring" would become the word "herring" in red). Do any of the words sound like other words that you can draw instead, like "I" and "eye?"

3 **BREAK THE WORDS DOWN INTO SYLLABLES,** and think of other ways they can be represented. For example, "catalog" could be shown with a picture of a cat, the letter "A," and a picture of a cut-down tree ("cat-a-log").

4 **LOOK FOR PREPOSITIONS, OR POSITIONING WORDS** like "in," "on," or "under." Often you can replace these with a visual clue by putting one word in, on, or under another: the letters "ALL" with a picture of the globe in between might mean "all around the world." Or instead of the word "back," write your clue in reverse: "SDRAW," for example, is "backwards."

5 **FIND A CLEVER FRIEND** and try your puzzles out on them—see how long it takes them to work out the answers.

Paradoxes

✦✦✦

Playing this game will not be any fun but *not* playing means you'll have a bad time. Will you have more fun playing or not playing the game? Before you try to answer the question, know that you've just read a paradox. A paradox is a statement or group of statements that seem to contradict themselves. Most of the time you can come up with a logical answer that will solve the dilemma presented in the paradox — even if that answer is to conclude that there *is* no satisfactory answer.

For example, here's a classic one, known as the liar's paradox: "This statement is false." Well, thinking about it you can eventually determine that the statement is both true and false, because if it's true then it must be false and if it's false then it must be true. Get it?

Sometimes paradoxes can be pictures or math problems as well as word games. They can play tricks on your normal thought processes and cause you to see things in a different light. Here are a few brain-teasers to get you started:

The paradoxical notice

Imagine you come across a sign saying "Please ignore this notice." Should you read it or shouldn't you? If you don't read it, how do you know to ignore it? And if you ignore it, how do you know not to read it?

The unexpected hanging

Imagine a prisoner. He is sentenced to death and has been told that he will be killed at dawn on one day of the following week. He has been assured that the day will be a surprise to him, so he will not be anticipating the hangman on a particular day, thus keeping his stress levels in check.

The prisoner starts to think to himself, "If I am still alive after dawn on Thursday, then clearly I shall be hanged on Friday, and this would mean that I know the day of my death in advance. Therefore I cannot be hanged on Friday. Now then, if I am still alive on Wednesday, then clearly I shall be hanged on Thursday, since I have already ruled out Friday — but that means Thursday's ruled out too. And if Thursday's ruled out, then if I'm alive on Tuesday I'll know Wednesday is the day, which rules out Wednesday . . ."

The prisoner works back with this logic through all the days of the week, finally concluding that he cannot after all be hanged, without already knowing which day it was. He sits back and relaxes, having decided that it's impossible for him to be hanged. The prisoner then gets a nasty shock on Tuesday when the warden arrives to take him away!

Explanation: This puzzle is a classic paradox, because each step of the prisoner's logic works. One way out of this is to say that the judge made a mistake, and that it is impossible for the day of the hanging to be a surprise to the prisoner. But the paradox takes a twist because the judge turns out to be right — the prisoner is surprised after all when the warden turns up on Tuesday!

Paradoxical pictures

It's also possible to use drawings to create a paradox. Often these work because the eye is tricked into viewing a two-dimensional object as a three-dimensional one. In the examples below, you can see that the third dimension doesn't always come out quite right, and that these shapes are in fact impossible.

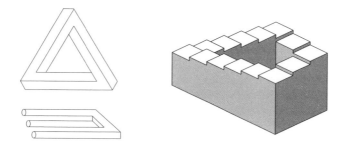

DID YOU KNOW? A Dutch artist called M.C. Escher specialized in drawing paradoxes like these. His pictures include staircases that are inside-out, water that appears to flow uphill, and houses where the normal rules of up and down just don't seem to apply.

Peg solitaire

Explorers who have eaten in a roadside diner during a family road trip probably know this board game. It usually comes in the shape of a wooden triangle with plastic pegs stuck in little holes on the board. The goal is to try to remove all but one peg from the board. You do this by jumping one peg over another into an open hole. Once a peg has been jumped over, you can remove it from the board.

Known as peg solitaire in England, this is a game that's at least 200 years old, with origins in France in the seventeenth century. It is sometimes played with marbles instead of pegs. The board and the pattern of pegs or marbles on it come in different shapes from different parts of the world. The shapes most commonly used are: a triangle in the US, with five pegs on each side; a diamond in Europe — actually more like a hexagon, with three pegs on each side; and a cross in Britain, with four squares of three pegs by three arranged around a single hole.

No matter where it's played, there is always one open hole to start the game off. That's usually in the middle of the board, except in the European version, where a hole in the middle of the board makes the puzzle impossible to solve.

To play, just jump one peg over another. Diagonal moving is not allowed. You can only jump over one peg at a time, and only if there's an empty space on the other side of the peg to jump into. Strategy is important because what you don't want to do is leave pegs standing alone. It's very difficult to reach a peg once it's been left behind.

You might be thinking this is an easy puzzle to solve, right? All you have to do is keep jumping pegs one over the other until you've only got one left. Trouble is, the peg that does the jumping can get stranded on its own away from other pegs, meaning you can never jump another peg over it to win the game.

DID YOU KNOW? The shortest number of moves to win at English peg solitaire (the one in the shape of a cross) is 18.

Mazes

✦ ✦

Like the giant mazes you walk through, a maze puzzle presents
you with an entry gate and an ending connected by confusing
passages and red herrings. It's up to you to find your way
through without getting hopelessly lost or stuck in a dead end.

Mazes can be simple, or so complicated that even Dad might have trouble solving
them. There are weave mazes, in which pathways can go over and under walls, and
puzzles that take the player through "holes" that lead to the back of the page
before returning to the front.

One technique you can use to find your way is called the "wall-follower"
technique. Usually, the walls or lines in a maze are connected from the entrance to
the exit. If you trace your pencil or finger along one side of a wall, you should
eventually find your way through. However, if the lines break up inside the maze,
this technique won't work.

Another technique you can use to get through a very complex maze is known as
Tremaux's algorithm. This is a way to rule out pathways as you come across them.
When you come to a junction, pick one path and mark both it and the path you just
came from. If you arrive at an already marked junction, then pick a path that isn't
marked and mark it as you go. If all the paths are marked, go down a marked path
but mark it a second time. Never take a path with two marks—any path marked
twice should be ruled out. It works every time—even if there is no exit to the maze,
this method will take you back to the entrance.

DID YOU KNOW? King Minos of Crete in ancient Greek legend built a
massive, unsolvable maze called a labyrinth underneath his palace to hold
the Minotaur, a monster half-man and half-bull. A young prince called
Theseus found his way through the maze using a ball of string given to him
by Minos' daughter to mark his way, and killed the Minotaur. The remains of
the palace were discovered in 1878, and there is a labyrinth of passages and
store-rooms buried beneath them. However, no evidence of the Minotaur has
been found . . . so far.

Word searches

❖

Word searches—those grids of letters with hidden words that you have to find and circle—are about as common as crossword puzzles, although a little easier to master. Rather than having a base of knowledge or an ability to decipher clues, you simply have to have a keen sense of observation to master these.

Most of them have themes that all the words play on. And you'll always have a list of words to choose from and cross out as you uncover them in the puzzle. Things get challenging when words are spelled backwards—which they often are in word searches. Diagonal, sideways, and horizontally written words are all allowed.

Creating your own word search

Once you've mastered the game, why not create one for your friends?

YOU WILL NEED

- A pen or pencil
- A ruler
- Paper

STEPS

1 FIRST, THINK UP A THEME and write down a list of words that fit with it. Then draw a grid on a piece of paper with a ruler. You can experiment with the number of squares, but start with 20 on each side.

2 GO THROUGH YOUR WORD LIST and write the words in the grid in various positions—horizontally, vertically, diagonally, and backward. You can write words across each other where they share the same letter.

3 WHEN YOU GET ALL YOUR WORDS in the grid (you may have to leave some out or add some, depending on whether you can fit them all in), fill in the remaining squares with random letters, and your puzzle is ready.

Treasure hunts

✦✦

No one gets tired of a good a treasure hunt, no matter how old they are. There's just something satisfying about picking up a map, deciphering the clues, and then running off to find the treasure at the end of the mystery.

Treasure hunts have been around for ages. There are lots of stories of pirates hiding their booty by burying it, and leaving cryptic or coded messages for their shipmates to help them track it down. One of the classics is *Treasure Island* by Robert Louis Stevenson, in which a young boy gets caught up in a quest for pirate gold. Not only do he and his companions have to find the island, they must decipher clues on the map to locate the treasure, and then face more pirates who want to claim the prize for themselves.

Creating a treasure hunt

You can use almost any of the puzzles in this chapter—riddles, paradoxes, logic puzzles, rebuses, and codes—for your clues. You can also use cryptic clues, like the ones you find in crosswords. These types of clues always contain a factual definition and some form of wordplay.

Because they take an active imagination and a sense of collaboration, treasure hunts should be played by teams of hunters so that everyone has to work together to get to the end.

YOU WILL NEED

- A pen or pencil
- Lots of paper
- Treasure
- A good hiding place

STEPS

1 THE KEY TO SETTING UP A SUCCESSFUL TREASURE HUNT is to start at the end. Decide what the prize is—a new compass, a pocket knife, a trip to the local theme park—and then decide where you're going to hide it.

2 THE BEST WAY TO MAKE UP YOUR HUNT is to work backward, so when you've hidden the treasure, write a clue that will help you find it.

3 USE THE PRINCIPLES FROM THE REST OF THIS CHAPTER to make your clue good and cryptic. Then find a good place to hide the clue, and think of another clue to lead your treasure-seekers to that place.

4 THINK UP FUN WAYS TO PRESENT CLUES. Write them on paper, hide them in boxes, rest them in nooks of tree branches, post them on a website, put them in a book at the library, wrap them in plastic and hide them in water, and so on. Make one clue a cryptic message that the participants won't be able to read until they find the decoder at the next stop.

5 WHEN EVERYTHING'S READY, get some treasure-seeking explorers together and give them the clue leading to the first hiding place (the last one you set up). Then let the fun begin!

Epilogue

If you've read this far, you've explored a lot already. Now it's time to get going on some exploration of your own.

The first Age of Exploration may have ended centuries ago, but new discoveries are still out there waiting for any boy curious enough to explore and master the worlds of science and the mind.

Index

A

acid indicator 21–2
air pressure 35
airfoil 52
airplane 52, 71
albatross 52
algorithm 130
anagram 134
anemometer 33
Arabic numerals 68
archeology 61, 62–5
asteroids 47

B

balloon
    fireproof 104–5
    pop-proof 103–4
    self-inflating 105
banana, pre-sliced 121
barometer 35
Battleships 144–5
bed of nails 115
Bernoulli's principle 52, 106
birds, flight 52
bishop's hat 91
boats
    density and floating 30
    magnet-powered 12–13
    soap-powered 14–15
bombs
    bubble 23–4
    smoke 36–7
    stink 102

bottle music 80–1
box, papier mâché 95
bubble bomb 23–4
bullet catch 116
butterfly 53–4

C

cabbage acid indicator 21–2
capillary action 32
car 69–71
carburetor 70
cards
    card trick 127
    solitaire 146–7, 148
Cartesian Diver 29–30
caterpillar 53–4
CD 43
cell-phone 44
central processing unit (CPU) 43
centrifugal force 110
chimpanzee 59
Chinese handcuffs 135
chlorophyll 55
chromatography 16–18
ciphers 130–1
clock 78–9
clock solitaire 148
codes 130–2
color 16–18, 45, 46
comets 47
compass 76–7
computer 42–3

operating system 42–3
    program 42
constructing 73–99
convection 39
crosswords 133–4
cryptic crosswords 133–4
cup and ball trick 122–123
cylinder (engine) 69–70

D

density 28–30, 39
diesel engine 71
digestion 22
dinosaur bones 64, 65
DVD 43
dyes 16–18

E

Earth 47, 48
    atmosphere 46
egg, turning into a mirror 25
electrical resistance 63
electricity, static 19–20, 76
engines 69–71
    diesel 71
    jet 71
    magnetic 13
    rocket 71
English Channel 75
ENIAC 43
Enigma code 131

Equator 66, 78
Escher, M.C. 152
excavation 64, 65
experiments 11–39

F
finger trap 135
fingerprints 58–9
flea circus 117
flight 52
flip book 114
football, table 85–7
fossils 64
friction 74

G
gas giant planets 48–9
generator 69
geophysics 63–4
geyser, soda 27
glass through a table
    111–12
gorilla 59
gravity 46
Gray Elephant from
    Denmark 125–6
Great Dark Spot 49
Great Red Spot 49
ground-penetrating radar
    (GPR) 64

H
hats, paper 90–2
helicopter 52
horsepower 71
hovercraft 74–5
Hughes, Howard 52

I
ice cube, picking up 26
ice hand 120
immiscible substances 39
Indian rope trick 115–16
internal combustion
    engine 69–70

J
jet engine 71
jigsaw puzzle 88–9
jug band 81
jumping ping-pong ball
    106
Jupiter 47, 48–9

K
kaleidoscope 83–4
Knights and Knaves 144
koala bear 59

L
latitude 66
lava lamp 38–9
leaves
    color change 55
    pressing 55–6
levitation
    olive 110
    teabag 109
lift, generating 52
light 45, 46
logic grids 140–1
longitude 66

M
Mad Hatter 92
magic tricks 101–27
magnetism 63–4

compass 76–7
magnet-powered boat
    12–13
Mars 47, 48, 51
mask, papier mâché 94–5
maze puzzles 154
Mercury 47
metamorphosis 53–4
meteorology 33, 35
Methuselah pine 57
Mexican jumping beans
    118–9
Mie scattering 46
military hat 92
mirrors
    hard-boiled egg 25
    kaleidoscope 83–4
misdirection 112
moons 47, 48
Morse Code 44
music
    bottle 80–1
    panpipes 82

N
Neptune 47, 48–9
Norse culture 137
number tricks 124–6

O
obelisk 79
oil
    immiscible with water
        39
    in engines 70
olive, levitating 110
optical illusions 113–14

P

paleontology 64
panpipes 82
paper hats 90–2
papier mâché 93–5
paradoxes 151–2
passwords 130–1
patience 54, 146–8
peg solitaire 153
permineralization 64
pH level 21–2
photocopier 20
photograph, magical 113–14
ping-pong ball, jumping 106
pirate hat 90–1
piston 69
planets 47–51
plaster casts 60–1
Pluto 47, 51
Pompeii 61
pond skater 15
postcard, putting your head through 107–8
pressure 115
prism 45
puppets 97–9
puzzles 129–57

R

radiation 45
radiator 70
rainbow 45
rebus 149–50
riddles 136–7
rocket engine 71
Roman numerals 67–8

S

Saturn 47, 48–9
scytale 132
shadow puppets 97–8
ship 30
sky, blue color 46
smell, testing sense of 31
smoke bomb 36–7
snake charming 116–17
soap-powered boat 14–15
sock puppets 98, 99
Socrates 41
soda geyser 27
solar system 47–51
modeling 50–1
soldier's hat 92
solitaire 146–7
clock 148
peg 153
sound vibrations 44, 80, 81
space exploration 51
Spruce Goose (airplane) 52
stars 47
static electricity 19–20, 76
stink bomb 102
submarine 13, 30
substitution codes 131
Sudoku 142–3
Sun 47, 78
sundial 78–9
supermagnet 13
surface tension 15

T

table football 85–7

tangrams 138–9
teabag, levitating 109
telegraph 44
telephone 44
Terracotta Army 65
theater, for puppets 99
Tolkien, J.R.R. 137
treasure hunts 156–7
tree, telling the age of 57
Tutankhamun's tomb 63

U

Uranus 47, 48–9

V

valerian root 102
Venus 47, 48, 51

W

Washington Monument 79
water
density and floating 28–30
immiscible with oil 39
moving uphill 32
water strider 15
Watt, James 71
wax 39
whirligig 96
wind speed 33–4
wings 52
word searches 155